The Most Amazing Basketball Stories of All Time for Kids

20 Inspirational Tales From

Basketball History for Young Readers

Bradley Simon

Table of Contents

Introduction

In the realm of sports, there exist battles of strength, contests of speed, and tests of endurance. However, basketball stands apart, a tantalizing blend of all these elements and more. The thump of the ball on the court, the echo of the buzzer, the swish of the net - these are the symphonies of the sport that captivate millions around the globe. This book aims to take you on a journey through the most interesting moments in basketball history. From its humble beginnings to its current status as a global phenomenon, each chapter presents a unique tale that has shaped the sport's landscape in unprecedented ways.

Basketball isn't just about throwing a ball into a hoop; it's a game of strategy, teamwork, and resilience, a testament to human spirit and potential. Each dribble, each pass, each shot has a story behind it. Sometimes, these stories are about overcoming adversity. At other times, they celebrate exceptional skill or teamwork. But always, they inspire us to reach for our dreams and never give up.

You'll dive into the early days of basketball, learning

about the creative mind of Dr. James Naismith, who, with simple peach baskets, birthed a sport that would resonate with countless generations. You'll step into the shoes of players who shattered records and redefined what it means to play the game. From Wilt Chamberlain's 100-point game to the Boston Celtics' miraculous comeback in 1969, these stories exemplify the awe-inspiring feats of athleticism and determination that define basketball.

You'll also explore the powerful narratives of teams that revolutionized the game and the rivalries that fueled them. Witness the evolution of the sport as the Harlem Globetrotters break racial barriers, and the Golden State Warriors redefine team play. Experience the titanic clash between Magic Johnson and Larry Bird, a rivalry that captivated fans and intensified the competitive spirit of the sport.

But this journey is not solely about the stars and the teams. It's about the moments that make the game, the pivotal points in history that shaped the trajectory of the sport. From the legendary Dream Team to Michael Jordan's legendary career, to the league-altering "Decision" by LeBron James, these chapters encapsulate the game-changing innovations and historic events that have kept basketball continually evolving.

Each chapter in this book is a testament to the rich

tapestry of basketball history, a nod to the heroes and moments that have shaped the game as we know it. As we embark on this journey, you'll come to understand why basketball is more than just a game. It's a story of triumph, heartbreak, innovation, and unity, an ongoing narrative that continues to inspire fans around the world.

So, grab your sneakers, young reader. It's time to step onto the court and delve into the most amazing stories in basketball history. Welcome to the game!

CHAPTER 1:

The Birth of Basketball: Dr. James Naismith's Peach Buckets

Once upon a time, in the small town of Almonte, Canada, lived a young boy named James Naismith. He loved to play outdoors, but the long, cold Canadian winters often kept him and his friends indoors. They yearned for a game they could play inside that was just as fun and energetic as their outdoor games. Little did James know that his childhood experiences would later inspire him to create one of the most popular sports in the world: basketball.

Fast forward a few decades to 1891. James Naismith was no longer a young boy. He was now a 30-year-old instructor at the International YMCA Training School in Springfield, Massachusetts. His job was to keep his students active during the winter while indoors. This was a tough task because winter in Massachusetts could be harsh, and most games they knew were suited for the outdoors.

One day, Dr. Luther Gulick, the superintendent of physical education at the school, gave Naismith a challenge. He asked Naismith to invent a new game that could be played indoors during the winter, a game that would be athletic and entertaining. It was a tall order. Naismith had to think outside the box to meet this challenge.

Naismith remembered his childhood in Canada and the games he used to play. He remembered the joy and energy of those games. He remembered the desire to play even when the winter chill kept them indoors. Naismith wanted to recreate that same joy and energy for his students. And so, he set out to invent a new game.

Naismith started by examining the popular games of the time—football, soccer, and rugby. But he found these games were too rough for indoor play. He wanted a game that involved skill more than strength, a game where contact would be limited to prevent injuries. With these considerations in mind, Naismith started to formulate the basic principles of his new game.

He decided that the ball should be big, so it would be easy

to handle. He decided that the goals should be elevated, so players would have to aim upwards, reducing the chance of collisions. And finally, he decided that the players should not be allowed to run with the ball, preventing the roughness found in other games.

Now, all Naismith needed was the equipment to play his new game. He asked the school janitor for two boxes, but the janitor came back with something else: two old peach baskets. They weren't exactly what Naismith had in mind, but they would work perfectly. Naismith took the baskets and hung them at the opposite ends of the gymnasium. He had his elevated goals.

With the peach baskets in place and a soccer ball in hand, Naismith was ready to introduce his new game. He scribbled down 13 basic rules, gathered his students, and basketball—though it wasn't named just yet—was born.

The students looked up at the hanging peach baskets and back at Naismith, puzzled. They had never seen a game like this before. Naismith explained the rules: they were to throw the ball into the opponent's peach basket to score points, but they couldn't run while holding the ball. They would have to pass it to their teammates to move it around. The team with the most points at the end of the game would be the winner.

The first game was a bit chaotic. Players had to get used to not running with the ball, and aiming the ball into the basket was harder than it seemed. Moreover, each time a player scored, someone had to climb up and retrieve the ball from the basket. But as they played, they started to understand the strategy and skill required. They realized how much fun it was.

Word of this new game spread quickly. It wasn't long before other YMCA centers started playing it too. And because the game could be played indoors, it became a popular activity for students during the winter months. Naismith's game was a hit!

Over time, the rules of the game were refined. The peach baskets were replaced with metal hoops and backboards, and a hole was added at the bottom so the ball could fall through. This saved a lot of time as no one had to climb up and get the ball out of the basket anymore. The soccer ball was replaced with a larger, more bounce-able ball. And Naismith's 13 basic rules evolved into the more detailed set of rules we know today.

But even as the game changed and evolved, the essence of what Naismith created remained. The game still required skill and strategy. It still promoted teamwork. And most importantly, it was still fun to play.

As the years passed, Naismith had the joy of watching his simple game grow and spread. It was played in high schools and colleges. It was played in public parks and playgrounds. It even became an official sport at the Olympics in 1936, with Naismith himself throwing the ceremonial first ball.

From a simple game invented to keep his students active during the winter, basketball had grown into a worldwide phenomenon. And it all started with a young boy's love for games, a teacher's creative thinking, and two old peach baskets.

In the years that followed, Naismith continued to be involved with the sport he created. He became a sports coach and athletic director, shaping the lives of many young athletes. He always emphasized the importance of sportsmanship and fair play. To him, these were as important as the skills needed to throw a ball into a basket.

As the popularity of basketball continued to grow, it began to take on a life of its own. The game evolved to fit into different cultures and settings. Kids in city playgrounds played on makeshift hoops, nailing rims onto telephone poles or backboards onto garage doors. Schools and community centers built proper basketball courts. Some places even started hosting basketball tournaments.

By the time of Naismith's death in 1939, basketball had become much more than a simple indoor game to keep his students active during winter. It was a sport that millions of people around the world loved and played. But more than that, it had become a vehicle for teaching important life skills, like teamwork, perseverance, and sportsmanship, just as Naismith had intended.

Even though Naismith is no longer with us, his legacy lives on in every bounce of the ball, in every swoosh of the net, and in every game played in driveways, school gyms, and professional arenas around the world.

Despite its humble beginnings, basketball has become one of the most popular sports in the world, and it continues to inspire and bring people together. From pick-up games at the local park to the high-stakes drama of the NBA Finals, the game of basketball is a testament to Naismith's ingenuity and his enduring impact on the world of sports.

Whether you're a player on the court making a critical pass, a coach devising strategies on the sidelines, or a fan cheering from the stands, the spirit of Dr. James Naismith is with you. Every time a player learns to dribble, every time a team works together to make a play, every time a young fan dreams of one day playing in the big leagues, Naismith's vision comes to life. It's a vision that started with a problem, a little bit of creativity, and two peach baskets. And it's a vision that continues to shape the world of sports today, more than a century later.

As we move through the chapters of this book and delve into the incredible moments, the awe-inspiring players, and the groundbreaking teams in basketball history, remember that it all started with a gym teacher, his students, and a simple game meant to keep those students active during a harsh winter. The birth of basketball is not just the start of a game; it's the start of countless stories of achievement, perseverance, and teamwork that continue to inspire us today.

CHAPTER 2:

Air Jordan: The Legend of Michael Jordan

O nce upon a time, in the bustling city of Brooklyn, New York, a star was born. His name was Michael Jordan, but little did he know, he would soon become one of the greatest basketball players in the world. His journey to the top wasn't easy, but his tale is a reminder that with hard work and determination, anything is possible.

When Michael was just a young boy, his family moved to Wilmington, North Carolina, a city that was mad about sports, especially basketball. Michael's father, James Jordan, built a basketball court in their backyard, sparking the young boy's interest in the game. He would spend hours out there, shooting hoops until the sun went down. The sound of the bouncing ball and the swish of the net were music to his ears, a melody that would stay with him for the rest of his life.

In high school, Michael tried out for the varsity basketball team. But, standing at only 5 foot 11, he was considered too short to play at that level and didn't make the team. Now, this could have been a crushing blow, but Michael didn't see it that way. Instead, he viewed it as a challenge. He practiced even harder, honing his skills and growing four inches over the summer.

By the time the next season came around, there was no ignoring his talent. Michael made the varsity team and quickly proved he was a force to be reckoned with on the court. But this was just the beginning of his journey. Soon, colleges from all over the country were knocking on his door, eager to recruit him.

After considering many offers, Michael decided to attend the University of North Carolina. There, under the guidance of Coach Dean Smith, he blossomed into a superstar. As a freshman, he made the game-winning shot in the 1982 NCAA Championship game against Georgetown. This moment was the first glimpse the world had of Michael's uncanny ability to perform under pressure, a trait that would become a hallmark of his career.

But even then, as the world began to take notice of his skill and prowess, no one could have imagined the heights that Michael Jordan would eventually reach. The best was yet to come.

After a successful three years at the University of North Carolina, which included an NCAA National Championship win in his freshman year in which he made the game-winning shot, Michael decided it was time to take the next step. He declared for the NBA draft, a decision that would change the landscape of basketball forever. In 1984, the Chicago Bulls selected him with the third overall pick. This was the moment Michael had been waiting for. He was ready to take the NBA by storm.

Right from the start, Michael made an impact. In his rookie season, he averaged an impressive 28.2 points per game and was named NBA Rookie of the Year. But that was just the appetizer. Michael was just getting warmed up.

His second season was marred by a broken foot, causing him to miss 64 games. But again, Michael didn't let adversity slow him down. He bounced back the following season, becoming the only player besides Wilt Chamberlain to score 3,000 points in a single season.

Michael's style of play was electrifying. He had a rare

combination of grace, power, speed, and an uncanny ability to score. He could soar through the air like a bird, earning him the nickname "Air Jordan". He would take off from the free-throw line and glide towards the basket, dunking the ball in a way that seemed to defy gravity. It wasn't long before his signature slam dunks were the stuff of legend.

But it wasn't just his talent that set him apart. It was his fierce competitiveness and unquenchable desire to win. Michael played every game as if it were his last. He hated to lose more than he loved to win, and it showed in every move he made on the court. Every dribble, every shot, every dunk was a testament to his relentless drive for success.

As Michael's fame grew, so did the popularity of the NBA. Fans all over the world tuned in to watch him play. He was a global sensation, and his influence on the game was immeasurable. But for all his individual success, there was one thing that eluded him - an NBA Championship. That, however, was about to change. The stage was set for Michael to lead the Bulls to an era of dominance that the NBA had never seen before.

As the 1990s dawned, the Chicago Bulls were on the cusp of greatness. They had a solid team, and at the center of it all was Michael Jordan. By now, he was known all over the world. Kids were wearing his jerseys and trying to replicate his moves on courts in their neighborhoods. He was a cultural icon, his influence reaching far beyond the bounds of basketball.

In the 1990-1991 season, the Bulls were unstoppable. They finished the regular season with the best record in the league. But the real challenge was the playoffs. It was a grueling journey, filled with high stakes and intense competition. But Michael and the Bulls were up for it. They powered through the playoffs, beating the Los Angeles Lakers in the finals to win their first NBA Championship.

The city of Chicago went wild. Thousands of fans poured onto the streets, cheering and celebrating their team's victory. For Michael, it was the fulfillment of a dream. He had reached the pinnacle of basketball success, and he was only just getting started.

Over the next eight years, Michael led the Bulls to a total of six NBA Championships, including two 'three-peats' - winning three championships in a row, twice! This was an astonishing feat, something that had only been achieved by a few teams in NBA history. Michael Jordan was not just a star; he was a legend.

However, it wasn't all smooth sailing. In 1993, Michael faced a personal tragedy when his father was murdered.

Shaken by his loss, he made a shocking decision - he retired from basketball to pursue a career in baseball, a sport his father loved. But after two years, he realized that his heart was still in basketball. In 1995, he made a dramatic return to the NBA with a simple press release stating, "I'm back."

His return was a major event. Fans were thrilled to see him back on the court, and he didn't disappoint. He picked up right where he left off, leading the Bulls to three more championships. His second 'three-peat' further solidified his status as one of the greatest players in the history of basketball. But as the 1990s came to a close, so did Michael's time with the Bulls. In 1998, after securing his sixth championship, Michael retired from the NBA for the second time.

But even in retirement, Michael Jordan's impact on the game continued. He had set new standards for what it meant to be an NBA player. His legacy was not just in the records he set or the championships he won, but in the way he played the game - with passion, determination, and a relentless desire to win. As we move on to the next chapter of our journey through basketball history, remember the legend of Michael Jordan. His story is a testament to what can be achieved with talent, hard work, and an unyielding will to succeed.

In 2001, Michael Jordan made headlines again, but this time, it wasn't about a retirement. No, Michael Jordan was returning to the NBA once more, but this time with the Washington Wizards. Fans were ecstatic, but they also had their concerns. After all, Michael was now 38, older than most players in the NBA. Could he still play at the level he was known for?

Well, if there was one thing Michael Jordan had shown throughout his career, it was that he thrived under pressure. He might have been older, but he was also wiser, and still had that same fiery competitiveness. His first season with the Wizards was impressive by any standards. He played in 60 games and averaged over 22 points per game. Not quite the same as his best years with the Bulls, but still remarkable, especially considering his age.

In his second season, however, Michael began to show signs of slowing down. He wasn't quite as quick on his feet, and his scoring average dropped. But even then, he was still a force to be reckoned with. He continued to inspire his teammates, pushing them to be better and showing them what it takes to compete at the highest level.

In 2003, after two seasons with the Wizards, Michael Jordan retired for the third and final time. His last game was on April 16, 2003, against the Philadelphia 76ers. Before the game, the 76ers presented Michael with a piece of the court from his high school in Wilmington, North Carolina. It was a touching tribute, a reminder of where it all began. As he walked off the court for the last time, the crowd gave him a standing ovation. It was a fitting end to an extraordinary career.

Michael Jordan's impact on basketball can't be overstated. He didn't just play the game, he transformed it. He set records, won championships, and became a global icon. His passion, skill, and competitive spirit made him one of the greatest players in the history of the sport. He was, and still is, Air Jordan, a legend who soared above the rest. The story of his career is one of determination, resilience, and an undying love for the game of basketball. His legacy continues to inspire players today, reminding us all that with hard work and dedication, the sky's the limit.

CHAPTER 3:

Breaking Barriers:

The Harlem Globetrotters and

the Integration of the NBA

O ur journey through basketball history now takes us to a team unlike any other, one that didn't just break records, but also broke barriers: The Harlem Globetrotters.

The story of the Harlem Globetrotters begins in the 1920s on the south side of Chicago, Illinois. Contrary to what their name might suggest, the Globetrotters didn't start in Harlem, New York. The team was actually formed by a man named Abe Saperstein, who decided to give them a name that would reflect the African American heritage of the players.

The Globetrotters started off as a serious competitive team, playing against local teams. But Saperstein quickly realized that his team had something special. They were naturally entertaining, often performing tricks with the basketball during games. So, he encouraged them to incorporate more of these antics into their play. The result was a unique blend of athleticism, theater, and comedy.

By the 1940s, the Globetrotters had gained considerable popularity. They were known for their exceptional basketball skills and their entertaining performances. But their influence extended beyond the court. They were breaking racial barriers at a time when segregation was still widespread in America. They were African American players traveling the country, and later the world, playing a game they loved while challenging racial stereotypes.

In the mid-1940s, the Globetrotters faced one of their biggest challenges yet: a match against the Minneapolis Lakers, who were considered the best team in the world at that time. This wasn't just any game; it was a showdown between the serious, professional Lakers and the fun-loving, trick-playing Globetrotters. The result? The Globetrotters emerged victorious, proving that they could hold their own against the best in the sport. This victory was a significant moment, not just for the Globetrotters, but for all African American players. It demonstrated that they had the talent and skill to compete at the highest level. The door to integration in the

NBA was starting to open.

The Globetrotters continued to play an important role in the integration of the NBA in the years that followed. In 1950, the NBA signed its first African American players, and one of them was a former Globetrotter: Nat "Sweetwater" Clifton. The Globetrotters had helped pave the way for this historic moment. And they didn't stop there. As they traveled the world, they continued to spread their message of unity and equality through the universal language of basketball.

Through their skill, charm, and tenacity, the Harlem Globetrotters showed the world that basketball is more than just a game. It's a platform that can be used to bring people together, challenge stereotypes, and inspire change. In our next section, we'll see how these pioneers of the sport were able to make a difference, both on and off the court.

As the Harlem Globetrotters gained fame and popularity, they didn't just captivate audiences with their entertaining style of play, they also began to captivate hearts and minds with their strength of character.

Remember, during the time when the Globetrotters were formed and began to rise to fame, racial segregation was the law of the land in many parts of the United States. Black and white people were kept separate in schools, restaurants, theaters, and even sports. Despite this, the Globetrotters, a team of all Black players, were traveling the country and playing in front of audiences that were often predominantly white.

Their games weren't just an exhibition of extraordinary basketball skills and entertaining antics, they were also a peaceful protest against segregation. When people saw the Globetrotters play, they weren't just seeing a basketball team. They were seeing a team of talented, charismatic, and dignified African American men challenging the stereotypes and prejudices of their time. The Globetrotters were demonstrating that excellence in sports—and indeed in any field—was not determined by the color of one's skin, but by talent, hard work, and dedication.

The Globetrotters' influence reached beyond the borders of the United States. As they began to tour internationally in the 1950s, they became ambassadors for both the sport of basketball and the idea of racial equality. They played in over 120 countries, bringing their unique brand of basketball to places like China, Russia, and even North Korea. In every country they visited, they left a lasting impression with their skill, showmanship, and goodwill.

Perhaps one of the most impactful moments in the Globetrotters' history occurred during their 1959 tour of the

Soviet Union. During the height of the Cold War, a period of intense rivalry and distrust between the United States and the Soviet Union, the Globetrotters played in Moscow's Lenin Central Stadium in front of a crowd of more than 14,000 spectators, including the Soviet leader Nikita Khrushchev. Despite the political tensions, the Globetrotters' game brought a moment of shared joy and humanity. The Russian crowd, who may have had preconceived notions about Americans, and particularly African Americans, were won over by the Globetrotters' skill and charm.

The Harlem Globetrotters were more than just a basketball team. They were pioneers, trailblazers, and ambassadors. Through their talent and charisma, they challenged prejudices, broke down barriers, and played a significant role in paving the way for the integration of the NBA. Their impact on the sport and on society is a testament to the power of sports as a force for change. As we move to the next chapter, we'll continue to explore the theme of breaking barriers, as we delve into the story of a basketball game that made history for a single player's extraordinary feat.

But how did the Harlem Globetrotters contribute to the integration of the NBA? This is a fascinating part of their story that is often overlooked.

In the mid-1940s, the NBA, which was then known as the

Basketball Association of America (BAA), was an all-white league. Despite the exceptional talent found in all-Black leagues and teams like the Harlem Globetrotters, the players of these teams were not given the opportunity to compete in the BAA due to the color of their skin.

The Globetrotters, however, were a team that could not be ignored. They were attracting large audiences, their games were exciting, and they were undeniably one of the best teams in the world. In fact, they were so good that in 1948, they were invited to play an exhibition game against the Minneapolis Lakers, who were then the BAA champions.

This was a game of immense significance. The Lakers, led by the towering George Mikan, were considered the best team in white professional basketball. The Globetrotters, led by the dazzling ball handler Marques Haynes and the versatile big man Reece "Goose" Tatum, were the champions of Black basketball. It was a contest that was about more than just basketball; it was about pride, representation, and the chance to challenge racial stereotypes.

The game was held at Chicago Stadium in front of an audience of over 17,000 spectators, making it one of the largest crowds to ever watch a professional basketball game at the time. For many in the audience, this was their first opportunity to see an integrated basketball game.

Against all odds, the Globetrotters won the game 61-59 in a nail-biting finish. This victory wasn't just a win for the Globetrotters; it was a win for all Black basketball players. It was a statement to the world that Black players were just as talented, if not more so, than their white counterparts.

This game was a turning point in the history of basketball. It opened the door for the integration of the NBA. Two years later, in 1950, Chuck Cooper became the first African American player drafted by an NBA team, the Boston Celtics. Shortly after, Nat "Sweetwater" Clifton, a former Harlem Globetrotter, signed with the New York Knicks, becoming the first African American player to sign an NBA contract.

The Globetrotters' victory against the Lakers had shown that Black players could compete at the highest level, and it had set the stage for the integration of the NBA. It was a landmark moment in the history of the sport and a testament to the role that the Harlem Globetrotters played in breaking down racial barriers.

The Globetrotters, with their blend of incredible skill, showmanship, and dignity, were not just entertainers, but also pioneers who helped change the face of basketball forever. As we continue our journey through the history of basketball, we'll find that this theme of breaking barriers and challenging norms is a recurring one, from the individual feats of extraordinary players to the evolution of the game itself.

CHAPTER 4:

Wilt Chamberlain's 100-Point Game:

A Record Never Broken

B asketball history is filled with spectacular moments, but few stand as tall as Wilt Chamberlain's astonishing 100-point game. In the early 1960s, Chamberlain was a phenomenon in the NBA. Towering at 7 feet 1 inch, he combined unprecedented height with outstanding skill, earning him a reputation as a formidable player for the Philadelphia Warriors.

It was March 2, 1962, when Chamberlain would leave his mark on sports history. That day, the Philadelphia Warriors were set to face the New York Knicks, in what many thought would be a routine game. Yet, as events unfolded, it became increasingly clear that this was no ordinary match.

Right from the opening whistle, Chamberlain was a man on a mission. His shots were finding their mark with uncanny consistency. He weaved through the defense, took off, and with a graceful arc, the ball sailed through the air and into the basket. Time and time again. By the end of the first quarter, Chamberlain had already amassed an impressive 23 points.

But he didn't stop there. As the game rolled on, so did Chamberlain's relentless scoring. He finished the first half with an incredible 41 points, a tally that many professional players would be proud to claim as a career high. As the teams retreated to the locker rooms for halftime, the question on everyone's lips was not if Chamberlain would continue his scoring spree, but just how high his tally might reach.

As the players returned to the court after halftime, the crowd's anticipation was palpable. Word had begun to spread about Chamberlain's extraordinary first half, and everyone was eager to see what the second half had in store. Even the opposing Knicks couldn't help but watch in awe as Chamberlain continued his unprecedented scoring onslaught.

Chamberlain played with an intensity that was rarely seen. He was unstoppable. His tall frame moved with the grace and agility of a dancer, effortlessly slipping past defenders and sinking shots from all angles. By the end of the third quarter, he had reached an unbelievable 69 points.

Meanwhile, in the crowd and across the airwaves, the atmosphere was electric. People were glued to their radios, hanging on to every word of the live commentary. The crowd in the stadium was on its feet, cheering every time Chamberlain scored. Even the game's referees found themselves caught up in the excitement, often shaking their heads in disbelief at the spectacle they were witnessing.

As the game entered its final quarter, Chamberlain was not just playing against the Knicks, but against the history of the game itself. His teammates began to feed him the ball at every opportunity, wanting to be a part of what was rapidly becoming a legendary moment in sports. The anticipation built with every point he scored. Could he really reach a hundred?

With just a few minutes remaining in the game, Chamberlain had scored 98 points. The arena was buzzing. Two more points and he would reach the unimaginable milestone. The Warriors had the ball, and naturally, they passed it to Chamberlain.

The Knicks tried to foul other players to keep the ball out of Chamberlain's hands, but the Warriors were determined. They got the ball to him, and as he rose above his defenders, time seemed to slow. The crowd held their breath as he launched the ball towards the basket.

Swish! It was in! The crowd erupted into cheers. Chamberlain had done it! He had scored 100 points in a single game, a feat no player in the NBA had ever achieved before. The game stopped temporarily as fans rushed onto the court to congratulate him. His teammates hoisted him onto their shoulders, and the crowd cheered his name.

Even today, Wilt Chamberlain's 100-point game is held in awe. Despite the many great players and incredible performances since then, no one has been able to match that feat. It remains a testament to Chamberlain's skill and a symbol of what can be achieved when someone pushes the boundaries of what is thought possible. This record stands as one of the most remarkable achievements in basketball history, a true testament to Chamberlain's dominance and skill in the sport he loved. It was a game, a night, a moment never to be forgotten.

In the days that followed, Chamberlain's 100-point game made headlines around the world. He was on the front page of every sports section, and even people who didn't follow basketball were talking about his remarkable achievement. Chamberlain himself was in a state of disbelief, humbled by the enormity of his accomplishment.

But this was more than just a personal achievement for Chamberlain. His 100-point game had a profound impact on the sport of basketball. It showed people the possibilities of the game, what a player could do with a basketball in their hands and the belief in their heart.

Basketball wasn't just a game of tall men passing and shooting a ball anymore. It was a spectacle, a show of athleticism, precision, and sometimes, a touch of the unbelievable. It was about breaking barriers and setting records. It was about making the impossible possible.

In the years that followed, many players would try to break Chamberlain's record. Some would come close, but no one has been able to reach the magical number of 100. Chamberlain's record has stood the test of time. It is a benchmark for greatness, a pinnacle that every scorer aspires to reach, and a constant reminder of that incredible night in Hershey, Pennsylvania.

As we close this chapter, remember Wilt Chamberlain's 100-point game as a testament to human potential. It shows us that records are made to be broken, that limits are meant to be pushed, and that with perseverance, determination, and a love for the game, anything is possible.

CHAPTER 5:

Magic vs. Bird: A Riveting Rivalry

It was a rivalry that transcended the basketball court. A clash of titans that captivated the nation and redefined the NBA. The names Magic Johnson and Larry Bird are synonymous with the golden age of basketball, and their rivalry is the stuff of legend.

Our story begins in the late 1970s, when basketball was struggling to gain mainstream popularity. Enter Earvin "Magic" Johnson, a charismatic point guard from Michigan State, and Larry Bird, a hardworking forward from Indiana State. Their paths first crossed in the 1979 NCAA Championship game, a showdown that would set the stage for one of the greatest rivalries in sports history.

Magic Johnson, with his flashy style and infectious smile, was the perfect foil to Bird's gritty determination and blue-collar work ethic. Their contrasting styles and personalities only added to the drama of their encounters. Magic was all about the razzle-dazzle, the no-look passes and the fast-break basketball. Bird, on the other hand, was a deadly shooter and a relentless rebounder, known for his clutch performances and fierce competitiveness.

In that NCAA final, Magic's Michigan State team emerged victorious, but this was just the beginning. Little did they know, they were destined to cross paths again and again, this time on the biggest stage of all - the NBA.

After that NCAA showdown, Magic and Bird entered the NBA as the first overall picks in consecutive drafts. Magic joined the Los Angeles Lakers in 1979, while Bird flew east to join the Boston Celtics in 1980. The Lakers were known for their 'Showtime' basketball - fast-paced, high-scoring games that were as entertaining as they were effective. The Celtics, on the other hand, prided themselves on their toughness, teamwork, and tenacity. The stage was set for an epic showdown.

Their first NBA encounter came in December 1979. The anticipation was palpable, and the game didn't disappoint. The Lakers, led by Magic's 23 points, edged out the Celtics in a thrilling encounter. But this was just a taste of the battles to come.

Throughout the 1980s, Magic and Bird met in the NBA Finals three times. Each series was a clash of styles, personalities, and coasts, with the laid-back Los Angeles lifestyle contrasting sharply with the blue-collar grit of Boston. It was Hollywood vs. the Heartland, Showtime vs. Substance.

In their first NBA Finals face-off in 1984, Bird's Celtics emerged victorious in a hard-fought seven-game series. Bird was named Finals MVP, but Magic would have his revenge.

In 1985 and 1987, Magic's Lakers claimed victory in the Finals against Bird's Celtics. Magic was named Finals MVP both times, cementing his place among the NBA's greats. Yet, despite the fierce rivalry on the court, a mutual respect developed between the two players. They pushed each other to new heights, with each one knowing that the other was the benchmark for greatness.

This rivalry wasn't just about Bird and Magic, though. It was about the Lakers and Celtics, two of the NBA's most storied franchises. It was about East Coast vs. West Coast, about different styles of basketball and different ways of life. And it was about the NBA itself, which saw its popularity soar during the Bird-Magic era.

As their careers progressed, Bird and Magic became

symbols of their respective franchises. Bird, with his blue-collar work ethic and relentless pursuit of victory, embodied the spirit of Boston. Magic, with his flashy passing, infectious smile, and love of the spotlight, was the perfect star for Hollywood's Lakers.

Their rivalry was one for the ages, a clash of titans that captivated basketball fans around the world. It was a rivalry filled with incredible performances, unforgettable moments, and high-stakes drama. But more than anything, it was a testament to the greatness of two of basketball's all-time legends: Larry Bird and Magic Johnson.

The Bird-Magic rivalry eventually extended beyond their playing careers. After retiring, both players went on to have successful careers in different roles within the NBA. Bird served as a coach and then as an executive for the Indiana Pacers, while Magic became a part-owner and executive of the Lakers.

Their impact on the game of basketball, however, was not limited to their contributions on the court or in the boardroom. The rivalry between Bird and Magic played a crucial role in popularizing the NBA globally, paving the way for the international success of the league today.

The Bird-Magic era also helped to change the way

basketball was played. Magic's showtime Lakers played a fast-paced, high-scoring style of basketball that was exciting to watch. Bird's Celtics, on the other hand, were known for their hard-nosed defense and team-oriented approach to the game. Both styles have had a profound influence on how the game is played and coached today.

In the end, the rivalry between Bird and Magic was about more than just basketball. It was about two remarkably different individuals pushing each other to the pinnacle of their sport, and in the process, transforming the game they loved. As the final buzzer sounds on this chapter, one thing is clear: the Bird-Magic rivalry was, and still is, one of the most riveting stories in the history of basketball.

And so, as we leave the courts where Bird and Magic once battled, we carry with us not only the memory of their spectacular games but also the lessons they taught us about competition, respect, and the sheer beauty of the game of basketball. The Bird-Magic rivalry will forever remain a golden chapter in the history of the NBA.

CHAPTER 6:

"The Decision": LeBron James

Shakes Up the NBA

The date was July 8, 2010, a day that would forever change the landscape of the NBA. All eyes were on LeBron James, arguably the most talented player in the league at the time. He was a free agent and was about to announce his decision on national television. Where would he play next?

LeBron James had been a sensation ever since he joined the NBA straight out of high school in 2003. Drafted by the Cleveland Cavaliers, he instantly became the face of the franchise. His electrifying dunks, pinpoint passes, and all-around dominance on the court won him fans all over the world. He was dubbed "The Chosen One" and was expected to bring a championship to his home state of Ohio.

However, despite his individual success, including winning two Most Valuable Player (MVP) awards, a championship eluded him in Cleveland. The team made it to the NBA Finals in 2007 but were swept by the San Antonio Spurs. After several more attempts to build a championship team around LeBron, the Cavaliers fell short. The 2009-10 season ended in disappointment, and LeBron's contract with the Cavaliers was up. Now, the entire sports world waited with bated breath. Would he stay, or would he go?

LeBron's decision was not just about where he would play basketball. It was also a massive event, the likes of which had never been seen in sports history. ESPN, a major sports network, scheduled a special live television program called "The Decision." LeBron would announce his choice on this show, with millions of people watching around the world. The anticipation was palpable.

Fans in Cleveland were on edge. They were hoping, praying that LeBron would stay. He was their hometown hero, born and raised in nearby Akron, Ohio. They could not bear the thought of him playing for another team. Meanwhile, fans of other teams fantasized about how LeBron could turn their fortunes around. The New York Knicks, Miami Heat, Chicago Bulls, and New Jersey Nets were all rumored to be in the running to sign LeBron.

Then the moment of truth arrived. LeBron, dressed in a checkered shirt, sat across from interviewer Jim Gray. Millions of viewers leaned closer to their television screens. After what seemed like an eternity, Gray asked the question everyone had been waiting for: "LeBron, what's your decision?" LeBron took a deep breath. He looked at Gray and said, "In this fall, this is very tough, in this fall I'm going to take my talents to South Beach and join the Miami Heat."

The reaction was immediate.

In Cleveland, fans were devastated. Some cried. Others were angry. Some even burned LeBron's jersey in the streets. They felt betrayed by their hometown hero. The owner of the Cavaliers, Dan Gilbert, wrote an open letter to fans, criticizing LeBron's decision and calling it a "cowardly betrayal."

In Miami, on the other hand, the mood was jubilant. Fans celebrated in the streets. The Miami Heat had not just acquired LeBron James, but also Chris Bosh, another top free agent. Together with Dwyane Wade, they formed a "super team." The Heat were immediately considered championship contenders.

LeBron's decision was met with a lot of criticism. Many people thought that the way he announced his move to Miami was disrespectful to Cleveland. Others felt that he took the easy route by joining a team with other superstars rather than trying to lead the Cavaliers to a championship himself.

Despite the criticism, LeBron's decision changed the NBA. It showed that players had the power to control their destinies and team up with other players to pursue championships. This has had a significant impact on the league, leading to the creation of other "super teams" in the years since "The Decision."

LeBron's move to Miami was indeed a shakeup, but it also taught a valuable lesson: decisions, even difficult ones, can lead to new opportunities and successes. Over the next four years, the Miami Heat would reach the NBA Finals four times, winning two championships. LeBron, once vilified for his decision, was now on top of the basketball world. And so, the story of LeBron James and "The Decision" serves as a reminder that sometimes, change, however hard it may be, can lead to greatness.

But the story of LeBron James didn't end with his success in Miami. After four seasons with the Heat, LeBron made another decision that would once again send shockwaves through the basketball world. In 2014, he decided to return to the Cleveland Cavaliers.

This time, there was no television special. Instead,

LeBron announced his decision in a heartfelt letter published in Sports Illustrated. He spoke about his love for Northeast Ohio, his desire to bring a championship to Cleveland, and his belief in the young Cavaliers team.

Back in Cleveland, the mood was completely different from what it had been four years earlier. The fans who had once burned his jersey in anger were now celebrating his return. They welcomed him back with open arms, hopeful that he could deliver the championship he had once promised.

Over the next few years, LeBron would lead the Cavaliers to the NBA Finals four times, just as he had done in Miami. But it was the 2016 championship that would be the most significant. Against the Golden State Warriors, one of the best teams in NBA history, the Cavaliers came back from a 3-1 deficit to win the series. It was the first major sports championship for the city of Cleveland in 52 years.

LeBron's story is one of redemption and resilience, of making difficult decisions and dealing with their consequences. His journey from Cleveland to Miami and back, from vilified to celebrated, is a testament to his character and his determination. It's a story that has left an indelible mark on the NBA, and it's a story that continues to unfold.

And as we close this chapter on LeBron James and "The

Decision," we're reminded that basketball is more than just a game. It's a journey filled with highs and lows, triumphs and setbacks. It's a journey that, like LeBron's, can take surprising turns and lead to unexpected destinations. And it's a journey that we, as fans, are privileged to witness.

CHAPTER 7:

The Golden State Warriors Dynasty:

Revolutionizing the Game

In the heart of Oakland, California, a revolution was brewing in the world of basketball. A team known as the Golden State Warriors was quietly building a dynasty that would not only dominate the sport but also redefine the way it was played.

The Warriors had long been a part of the NBA, but they had mostly been a middling team, with only a few bright spots in their history. That all changed in the 2010s when a talented group of players came together and started to transform the Warriors into a powerhouse.

The transformation began with a player named Stephen Curry. Drafted by the Warriors in 2009, Curry was an exciting player with a phenomenal shooting touch. His ability to make three-point shots from anywhere on the court was breathtaking, and it quickly earned him the nickname "Chef Curry" because he was always "cooking" up something special on the basketball court.

But Curry wasn't the only player who made the Warriors special. There was also Klay Thompson, another outstanding shooter who could catch fire at any moment and rain down three-pointers on the opposition. Together, Curry and Thompson became known as the "Splash Brothers," turning games into dazzling shooting exhibitions.

This Splash Brothers duo, with their deep range and quick release, was just the beginning of the Warriors' revolution. They were soon joined by a versatile forward named Draymond Green. While Green wasn't a scoring machine like Curry or Thompson, he brought a different kind of magic to the court. He was an excellent defender, able to guard almost any player on the opposing team. But what set him apart was his ability to make plays for his teammates. He could grab a rebound, then quickly turn and throw a long pass down the court to a sprinting Curry or Thompson for an easy basket.

The Warriors' style of play, which emphasized fast breaks, three-point shooting, and ball movement, was a dramatic shift from the traditional, slower-paced game. This style, which became known as "small ball," relied on smaller, more versatile players who could run fast, shoot from distance, and switch roles quickly.

The transformation of the Warriors was accelerated in 2014 when Steve Kerr took over as head coach. Kerr, a former NBA player and champion himself, had a deep understanding of the game. He immediately recognized the potential of the Warriors' roster and implemented an offensive system that maximized their talents. Under Kerr's guidance, the Warriors' free-flowing, fast-paced style of play became even more potent, and their success started to skyrocket.

The Warriors' dominance was not just due to their exceptional players and innovative tactics; it was also fostered by a culture of unity and mutual respect. Coach Steve Kerr fostered a positive, inclusive atmosphere, where every player, regardless of their role, felt valued. This created a strong team spirit, where players were willing to sacrifice individual glory for the success of the team.

In the 2014-15 season, the Warriors' unique approach bore fruit as they won an impressive 67 games in the regular season. They sailed through the playoffs and, in the NBA Finals, they faced off against LeBron James and the Cleveland Cavaliers. But even the mighty LeBron could not halt the Warriors' charge. The Warriors won the series 4-2, securing their first NBA Championship in 40 years.

The following season, the Warriors broke another record. They won an astonishing 73 games in the regular season, beating the previous record set by the 1995-96 Chicago Bulls - a team that included the legendary Michael Jordan. However, despite this incredible achievement, the season ended in heartbreak as the Warriors lost to the Cavaliers in a thrilling seven-game Finals series.

Yet, the Warriors weren't done. In the 2016 offseason, they added another superstar to their roster - Kevin Durant. With Durant joining the team, the Warriors had formed a "super team," and they went on to win two more NBA Championships in 2017 and 2018. The Golden State Warriors had not only revolutionized the game with their style of play but also set a new standard for team construction in the NBA. The dynasty they built in the mid-2010s will be remembered as one of the most dominant in NBA history.

However, like all great things, the Warriors' reign had to come to an end. In the 2018-19 season, they faced numerous challenges. Injuries began to take their toll, and the team dynamics seemed to be shifting. Nevertheless, the Warriors powered through and once again found themselves in the NBA Finals, this time against the Toronto Raptors.

The Raptors were a formidable team, led by the calm and composed Kawhi Leonard. Despite the Warriors' best efforts, the Raptors had an answer for everything. In a hard-fought series, the Raptors emerged victorious, ending the Warriors' two-year reign as NBA champions.

Following this loss, the Warriors entered a period of transition. Kevin Durant left the team for the Brooklyn Nets, and key players like Klay Thompson and Steph Curry faced significant injuries. The team that had once seemed invincible was suddenly vulnerable.

Yet, the legacy of the Warriors' dynasty continues to influence the NBA. Teams across the league have tried to replicate their success by building their own "super teams" and adopting a similar style of play. The Warriors' emphasis on three-point shooting, ball movement, and positional versatility has become the standard in modern basketball.

The Golden State Warriors' dynasty was a period of unprecedented success and innovation. It was a time when a team dared to challenge conventional basketball wisdom and, in doing so, revolutionized the game. The impact of this remarkable team will be felt in the NBA for years to come, a testament to their dominance and the indelible mark they left on the sport of basketball. And so ends the story of the Golden State Warriors' dynasty, a thrilling tale of innovation, success, and the relentless pursuit of greatness.

CHAPTER 8:

The Miracle of 1969: The Boston Celtics' Unbelievable Comeback

In the world of sports, there are moments that simply defy belief, moments that make you question the very fabric of reality. One such moment occurred in 1969, in the heart of the NBA. The Boston Celtics, one of the most storied franchises in the league, found themselves in a nearly impossible situation. But they also found the strength to pull off one of the greatest comebacks in basketball history.

It was the NBA Finals, and the Celtics were facing off against the formidable Los Angeles Lakers. The Lakers were a team of superstars, boasting the talents of Jerry West, Elgin Baylor, and the recently acquired Wilt Chamberlain, one of the most dominant players in the history of the sport. On paper, the Lakers seemed unstoppable.

The Celtics, on the other hand, were not the same team that had won 10 of the last 12 NBA Championships. Their legendary coach, Red Auerbach, had retired, and their star player, Bill Russell, was nearing the end of his career. Many thought the Celtics' era of dominance was over, and their chances of winning another title were slim at best.

The Lakers quickly took control of the series, winning two of the first three games. The Celtics were on the ropes, facing a Lakers team that seemed to be at the peak of its powers. But the Celtics were not ready to go down without a fight. They dug deep, found their resolve, and managed to tie the series at 2-2. However, the Lakers struck back in Game 5, bringing the series to 3-2 in their favor. Now, the Celtics were one loss away from defeat. The situation was grim.

With their backs against the wall, the Celtics had to win Game 6 on their home court to keep their championship hopes alive. And win they did, pulling out all the stops to secure a crucial victory that sent the series back to Los Angeles for a decisive Game 7. It was all or nothing now, and the tension was palpable.

As the teams took the court for Game 7, the noise of the Los Angeles crowd was deafening. The Lakers' fans were expecting a victory parade, but the Celtics had other plans. The game was a nail-biter from the start, with both teams trading leads multiple times. The Celtics fought tenaciously, showing the heart and determination that had won them so many championships in the past.

In the final minutes, the Celtics clung to a narrow lead. Every possession mattered, every shot could make the difference. With just seconds left, the Lakers had the ball and a chance to win the game. The crowd held its breath as Jerry West took a shot... and missed. The Celtics had done it! They had pulled off an incredible upset to win the championship.

But the real miracle wasn't just the victory, it was the manner in which it was achieved. The Celtics had been written off by many, expected to bow out gracefully to the mighty Lakers. But they refused to accept defeat, instead choosing to fight for every point, every rebound, every loose ball. Their miraculous comeback wasn't just a testament to their skill, but to their heart, their grit, and their refusal to give up, even when the odds were stacked against them.

And so, the Miracle of 1969 was etched into the NBA history books, a tale of perseverance and determination that continues to inspire basketball players and fans alike to this very day. After the game, an emotional Bill Russell, who had also been the team's coach, hoisted the championship trophy high into the air, a symbol of a victory that no one saw coming, a victory that defied all odds. But as he looked out at his teammates, he knew that it was their belief in each other, their unyielding spirit, that had truly won the day.

A celebration erupted in the Celtics' locker room, a mix of elation, relief, and a dash of disbelief. Bill Russell, the player-coach, was at the center of it all, having led his team to an improbable victory with a performance that was nothing short of heroic.

But amidst the laughter and cheers, Russell took a moment to remind his team of the importance of their achievement. "We didn't just win a game," he said, his voice rising above the din, "we won because we never stopped believing in ourselves. We won because we played as a team. We won because we refused to be defined by what others thought we could or couldn't do."

That victory in 1969 was more than just another championship for the Boston Celtics. It was a testament to the power of belief, teamwork, and resilience. It was a reminder that, in basketball as in life, the game isn't over until the final buzzer sounds. And most importantly, it was a lesson that, no matter how insurmountable the odds may seem, miracles can, and do, happen.

The story of the 1969 Celtics is not just about a stunning basketball game, but also about the spirit of the sport. Each player on that team - Bill Russell, Sam Jones, John Havlicek, Don Nelson, and the rest - were heroes that night, but more importantly, they were teammates. They each played their part, recognizing that they had a role to play and a contribution to make.

They didn't just play for themselves, they played for each other. They played for the city of Boston, for their fans, and for everyone who believed in them. When they were down, they didn't crumble under the pressure. Instead, they rose to the occasion, showing the world what it means to be a team.

And isn't that what sports is all about? It's about pushing your limits, about working together, about never giving up no matter how difficult things get. It's about the thrill of the game, the roar of the crowd, and the satisfaction of knowing you gave it your all. It's about the lessons we learn, the friendships we make, and the memories we create.

So as we close the chapter on the Miracle of 1969, let's remember the Boston Celtics not just as champions, but as a symbol of the power of teamwork, perseverance, and belief. Their story is a reminder that in basketball, and in life, we should never stop dreaming, never stop trying, and never stop believing in the power of "us". For when we come together, who knows? We might just create a miracle of our own.

As the years passed, the story of the 1969 Celtics and their miracle comeback became the stuff of legend. Bill Russell retired after the championship win, but his legacy lived on, inspiring new generations of Celtics and basketball players all over the world.

The Miracle of 1969 was a defining moment in the NBA, and it serves as a timeless reminder of what can be achieved when we refuse to give up, even in the face of the greatest challenges. So next time you're watching a basketball game and the odds seem to be stacked against one team, remember the Celtics' miraculous comeback. After all, as the 1969 Celtics showed us, in basketball, anything is possible.

CHAPTER 9:

Reggie Miller vs. The New York Knicks:

A Clutch Performance

The date was May 7, 1995. The place? Madison Square Garden, New York City. It was Game 1 of the Eastern Conference Semifinals, pitting the Indiana Pacers against the New York Knicks. The Knicks were leading by 6 points with only 18.7 seconds left on the clock. It seemed like a sure win for the New Yorkers. But Reggie Miller, the sharpshooting guard for the Pacers, had other plans.

Reggie Miller wasn't just any basketball player. He was known for his clutch performances and ability to sink three-pointers with ease. He had a knack for turning up the heat when it mattered most. But even his standards, what happened next was extraordinary.

The Pacers inbounded the ball to Miller. He quickly hit a three-pointer, cutting the Knicks' lead to just 3 points. The Madison Square Garden crowd went silent. They could feel something brewing. But no one could have predicted what came next. The Knicks inbounded the ball, but Miller, in a sneaky move, stole the pass. He dribbled back behind the three-point line and released the ball. Swish. Another three-pointer. The game was tied. The crowd was stunned. Miller had scored 6 points in just 3.1 seconds!

But he wasn't done yet. The Knicks missed their next shot, and Miller was fouled while grabbing the rebound. He stepped up to the free throw line and coolly made both shots, bringing his total to 8 points in 8.9 seconds. The Pacers took the lead, and the crowd was left in disbelief.

The buzzer sounded, and the Pacers celebrated their victory. Reggie Miller had pulled off one of the greatest clutch performances in NBA history. His incredible feat is still remembered today as a testament to his skill, determination, and sheer will to win. It was a magical moment in basketball history, a reminder that in this game, it's never over until the final buzzer sounds. And it was a lesson in the power of belief, in oneself and in one's team, that continues to inspire basketball players around the world.

News of Miller's miraculous performance spread like

wildfire. The next day, newspapers and sports shows all over the country were talking about "Miller Time." His quick thinking, precise shooting, and gritty determination had turned the tide of the game in a way that seemed impossible. It instantly became an iconic moment in NBA history, not just for its stunning execution, but also for its significance in the broader context of the Pacers-Knicks rivalry.

You see, the Pacers and the Knicks had a history of intense playoff battles. In the previous year, during the 1994 Eastern Conference Finals, the Knicks had edged out the Pacers in a hard-fought seven-game series. Miller had played exceptionally well, even scoring 25 points in the fourth quarter of Game 5, but it wasn't enough to secure the Pacers a spot in the NBA Finals.

This loss was still fresh in the Pacers' minds as they entered the 1995 playoffs. Miller, in particular, was eager to avenge their defeat. He was known for his competitive spirit and never-back-down attitude. These traits were on full display in his incredible 8-point flurry in Game 1, which served as a statement to the Knicks and the rest of the NBA: the Pacers were here to compete, and they wouldn't go down without a fight.

Miller's stunning performance did more than just win the Pacers a game. It changed the momentum of the series. The

Pacers went on to win the series 4 games to 3, finally overcoming their rivals and making it to the Eastern Conference Finals. Miller's incredible 8-point outburst had turned the tide, providing the spark that propelled the Pacers to victory.

The story of Reggie Miller's clutch performance against the Knicks is a thrilling tale of determination, skill, and the power of never giving up, even when the odds seem stacked against you. It's a story that resonates with basketball fans of all ages, reminding us all that in the game of basketball, anything is possible.

CHAPTER 10:

The International Impact: Dirk Nowitzki, Manu Ginobili, and Yao Ming

Basketball is a game that knows no borders. It is loved and played in every corner of the globe, but this wasn't always the case. There was a time when the NBA, the most prestigious basketball league in the world, was almost entirely made up of American players. That all started to change, however, with the arrival of some extraordinary talents from overseas.

Imagine being a kid in Germany, spending countless hours shooting hoops in your backyard, dreaming of one day playing in the NBA. This was the reality for a young Dirk Nowitzki. Born in Würzburg, Germany, Dirk fell in love with basketball at a young age. He would spend hours honing his skills, practicing his shooting, and dreaming of playing in the NBA.

As he grew, so did his talent. Standing 7 feet tall, Dirk had a rare combination of size and skill that made him a unique player. He had the height of a center, but the shooting touch of a guard. This blend of abilities drew the attention of NBA scouts, and in 1998, Dirk's dream came true when he was drafted by the Dallas Mavericks.

Across the ocean in Argentina, another future NBA star was making his mark. Manu Ginobili grew up in a basketball family. His older brothers played professionally in Argentina, and Manu was eager to follow in their footsteps. Known for his fiery competitiveness and unorthodox style of play, Manu quickly became a standout player in Argentina. In 1999, he was drafted by the San Antonio Spurs, becoming only the second player from Argentina to make it to the NBA.

Over in China, a young center named Yao Ming was dominating the Chinese Basketball Association. Standing at a towering 7 feet 6 inches, Yao was an imposing figure on the court. But he was more than just tall. Yao had a soft touch around the basket and a keen understanding of the game. His talent was undeniable, and in 2002, Yao was selected as the first overall pick in the NBA Draft by the Houston Rockets.

Dirk, Manu, and Yao all faced challenges adjusting to the NBA. The game was faster, the competition tougher, and the pressure immense. But they persevered, and in doing so, they didn't just become great players, they became ambassadors for the game of basketball, paving the way for future generations of international players.

Each of these international stars had a significant impact on the game and their respective teams. Dirk Nowitzki became the face of the Dallas Mavericks and revolutionized the power forward position with his outside shooting ability. He led the Mavericks to their first NBA Championship in 2011 and became the first European player to be named the NBA Finals Most Valuable Player (MVP). Dirk's success opened the door for other European players, proving that they could not only compete in the NBA but also be among its biggest stars.

Meanwhile, in San Antonio, Manu Ginobili was turning heads with his flashy style of play. Known for his creative passes and daring drives to the basket, Manu became a fan favorite in San Antonio. Alongside teammates Tim Duncan and Tony Parker, Manu helped the Spurs win four NBA Championships. His success inspired a generation of players in Argentina and Latin America, showing them that they too could make it to the NBA.

In Houston, Yao Ming was making a name for himself as

one of the league's top centers. Despite facing initial skepticism, Yao quickly proved he belonged in the NBA. He was an 8-time All-Star and became one of the most dominant centers in the game. But perhaps more importantly, Yao's success sparked a basketball frenzy in China. His games were watched by millions of fans in his home country, and he helped introduce the NBA to a massive new audience.

These players didn't just change the game; they helped globalize it. Thanks to Dirk, Manu, and Yao, the NBA became a more diverse and international league. Today, it's common to see players from all over the world shining in the NBA. But we can't forget the trailblazers who helped make this possible. So, as we watch the latest international stars light up the court, let's remember the impact of Dirk Nowitzki, Manu Ginobili, and Yao Ming. They showed the world that basketball truly is a global game. And that's something worth celebrating!

The impact of these international stars extended beyond the court, into the realms of culture and commerce. Nowitzki's success in Dallas didn't just make headlines in the United States, but also in his native Germany. Basketball camps, clinics, and leagues sprouted up across the country as children and teens were inspired by Dirk's achievements. The NBA's popularity soared in Germany, and basketball started to challenge soccer's reign as the nation's favorite sport.

In Argentina, the situation was similar. Manu's daring plays and energetic style were contagious, and his success with the San Antonio Spurs captivated his home nation. Streets and parks in Argentina filled with youngsters eager to replicate Manu's moves, and the sport's popularity skyrocketed. Thanks to Manu, Argentina became a powerhouse in international basketball competitions.

China's relationship with basketball transformed with Yao's rise to stardom. His games were broadcast nationally, and millions of people tuned in to watch him play. Yao's impact was so profound that the NBA started hosting games in China to cater to the country's booming interest in basketball. This helped the NBA tap into a vast new market, expanding its global reach significantly.

The achievements of Nowitzki, Ginobili, and Yao marked a turning point in the NBA's history. Their success not only proved that international players could compete at the highest level but also that the sport of basketball had global appeal. Their influence continues to be felt today, as an increasing number of international players enter the NBA, bringing with them unique styles of play and further globalizing this incredible game.

CHAPTER 11:

Bill Russell and the Boston Celtics:

A Dynasty of Defense

During the late 1950s and 1960s in Boston, Massachusetts, a basketball revolution was brewing. It was not only a revolution in the way the game was played, but also a transformation in how defense was understood. This revolution was led by a towering figure, both in stature and influence - Bill Russell.

Russell was born in 1934 in Monroe, Louisiana, during a time of significant social unrest and racial segregation. Despite the challenges he faced growing up, basketball became his refuge. He spent countless hours on the court, honing his skills, and dreaming of a future where he could play the game he loved professionally.

His journey to the Boston Celtics wasn't straightforward. Russell first made his mark at the University of San Francisco, where he led the team to two consecutive NCAA championships in 1955 and 1956. His extraordinary ability to block and alter shots, combined with his rebounding prowess, set him apart from his peers. However, it was his understanding of the game, his leadership, and his ability to inspire his teammates that truly made him unique.

After his impressive college career, Bill Russell was selected as the second overall pick in the 1956 NBA draft by the St. Louis Hawks. However, he would never play a game for them. In a bold move, the Boston Celtics' coach, Red Auerbach, orchestrated a trade that brought Russell to Boston. Auerbach had seen something special in Russell, something that he believed could transform the Celtics into a championship team. He was right.

Russell joined the Celtics in December 1956, after he had finished playing for the United States in the Melbourne Olympic Games, where he won a gold medal. He quickly established himself as a defensive powerhouse in the NBA. In his rookie season, Russell averaged an astonishing 19.6 rebounds per game, helping the Celtics to their first NBA championship in 1957.

Russell was not the typical center. He wasn't always the

highest scorer, but he dominated the game in other ways. He was an incredible rebounder, using his 6'10" frame and exceptional leaping ability to control the boards. But it was his shot-blocking that truly set him apart. Russell had an uncanny ability to time his jumps and swat the ball away just as his opponents were trying to score. His defensive prowess often turned into offensive opportunities for the Celtics, as Russell was also a skilled passer, frequently starting fast breaks with his defensive rebounds or blocked shots.

But what truly made Russell a revolutionary player was his understanding of team defense. He knew that defense wasn't just about blocking shots. It was about communication, about helping teammates, and about intimidating and frustrating the opposition. He was the anchor of the Celtics' defense, directing his teammates and making adjustments based on the flow of the game. His ability to read the game and make the right defensive play was unparalleled, and it turned the Celtics into the best defensive team in the league.

The impact of Russell's defensive genius was felt immediately throughout the league. Teams had to adjust their strategies when they faced the Celtics. Opposing players found it difficult to score when they were up against Russell, and this had a profound effect on games. But what was perhaps even more significant was how Russell's style of play started to change the way defense was viewed and valued in basketball.

Before Russell, basketball was a game largely focused on offense. Players were primarily judged by their scoring ability. Defense was often an afterthought. But Russell demonstrated that defense could be just as important as offense, if not more so. His tenacious and intelligent defensive play was a key factor in the Celtics' success, and it wasn't long before other teams started to pay more attention to defense.

Russell's influence extended beyond the NBA. He changed the perception of the center position. Traditionally, centers were expected to be high scorers and dominant offensive players. But Russell showed that a center could be the key defensive player on a team, protecting the basket and controlling the paint. This had a lasting impact on the game of basketball. Future generations of players who excelled defensively, particularly centers, would often be compared to Russell.

Under Russell's leadership, the Celtics developed a reputation for being a tough, defensive-minded team. They weren't always the most flashy or high-scoring team, but they were incredibly effective. The Celtics' style of play, which emphasized teamwork, defense, and winning above all else, became a blueprint for success in basketball. The team's emphasis on collective, rather than individual, success was embodied in Russell, who once said, "The most important measure of how good a game I played was how much better I'd made my teammates play."

Russell's remarkable career was not only marked by his unique style of play but also by his pioneering spirit. He was one of the first African American players to achieve superstar status in the NBA, and he faced considerable racial prejudice both on and off the court. But Russell remained undeterred and continued to break barriers throughout his career.

In 1966, he made history by becoming the first African American coach in any major professional sport in the United States. The Celtics appointed him as their player-coach, and under his leadership, they won two more NBA championships. This was a significant achievement, not just for Russell and the Celtics, but for the entire NBA and the sport of basketball. It signaled a significant step forward in racial equality in sports and the wider society.

When Russell retired in 1969, he left an indelible mark on the sport of basketball. His 11 championship rings are the most in NBA history. But perhaps more importantly, his influence on the game went far beyond his individual accolades. He helped redefine the game of basketball, placing a greater emphasis on defense, teamwork, and collective success. His impact on the sport can still be felt today, with many modern players and teams emulating his defensive prowess and team-first mentality.

Thus, the story of Bill Russell and the Boston Celtics is not just a tale of one player or one team's success. It's a story of how the game of basketball evolved and changed. It's a story of breaking barriers and overcoming adversity. But most of all, it's a story of how a player who valued defense and teamwork above all else could lead his team to the pinnacle of success, time and time again. Through his incredible career, Bill Russell truly established a Dynasty of Defense. And with that, we conclude the story of this amazing era of basketball.

CHAPTER 12:

The Dream Team: Basketball's Best Assemble for the Olympics

The year was 1992, and the stage was set in Barcelona, Spain, for the Summer Olympics. Basketball, a sport invented in America, had gained popularity around the world, but it was at this event that its international stature would ascend to unprecedented heights. The reason? The creation of an American team so spectacular, so laden with talent, it would come to be known as the "Dream Team."

The International Basketball Federation (FIBA) had just allowed professional NBA players to participate in the Olympics. This decision paved the way for the United States to assemble a team that was nothing short of a basketball fantasy brought to life. The Dream Team comprised the crème de la crème of the NBA, including the likes of Michael Jordan, Magic Johnson, Larry Bird, and Charles Barkley, among others. These were players who had dominated the NBA in the 1980s and early 1990s and were now about to showcase their prowess on a global stage.

The Dream Team was a fusion of dazzling individual talent and collective mastery. Each player was a superstar in his own right, but together, they formed a team that was simply unmatched. From the moment they stepped onto the court, it was clear that they were in a league of their own. The world watched in awe as they glided past opponents with ease, displaying an extraordinary level of skill, finesse, and teamwork.

This chapter will delve into the creation of this team, their journey through the Olympics, and the lasting impact they had on the sport of basketball globally. It's a tale of talent, teamwork, and the dazzling heights that can be achieved when the best in the game come together for a common goal. It's the story of the Dream Team.

Assembling the Dream Team was an endeavor in itself. The selection process was rigorous, aiming to create not just a group of all-stars, but a cohesive unit that could seamlessly play together. The committee chose a perfect blend of veterans and young stars, offensive powerhouses, defensive giants, and players known for their ability to create opportunities for others. The final roster was an exhibition of basketball finesse, an exhibition that the world had never seen before.

The team was led by head coach Chuck Daly, who had the task of managing this colossal pool of talent. Daly, having coached the Detroit Pistons to two consecutive NBA championships, was an apt choice. His calm demeanor, strategic acumen, and ability to manage egos were key in molding this set of superstars into a well-oiled machine.

The Dream Team's journey in the Olympics was a spectacle to behold. They sailed through the tournament, effortlessly winning every game. The world watched in awe as they took the court, scoring at will and defending with tenacity. Their style of play was rapid, their ball movement fluid, and their shooting accuracy pinpoint. They won their games by an average margin of 44 points, a testament to their sheer dominance.

The gold medal match against Croatia was a fitting conclusion to their campaign. The Dream Team showcased their best basketball, defeating the Croatian team 117-85. The final whistle marked the end of a campaign that had mesmerized the world, solidifying the Dream Team's place as one of the most dominant squads ever assembled in any sport. Their gold medal was a symbol of their unmatched prowess and the culmination of a journey that had captured the world's imagination.

The Dream Team's impact extended far beyond their triumphant Olympic journey. Their excellence on the court, the style with which they played the game, their camaraderie, and their global appeal had a profound impact on the sport of basketball.

The Dream Team captured the attention of the international community, propelling the popularity of basketball to new heights across the globe. Their games were watched by millions of people worldwide, many of whom were witnessing the sport at its finest for the first time. This exposure played a significant role in inspiring a new generation of players outside the United States, leading to an influx of international talent in the NBA in the subsequent years.

Off the court, the Dream Team was equally influential. They were not just basketball players; they were global icons. The charisma of Magic Johnson, the competitive spirit of Michael Jordan, the quiet leadership of Larry Bird, and the unique styles of Charles Barkley, Karl Malone, and the others made them universally admired figures. They were role models for aspiring athletes, showing the world that basketball was more than just a game - it was a medium to express oneself, to create, and to inspire.

Basketball, as a global sport, owes much to the Dream Team. Their presence at the Olympics was a pivotal moment in the sport's international expansion. The games were broadcasted around the world, capturing the imagination of millions of viewers. Many young people, enthralled by the spectacle, picked up a basketball for the first time and dreamt of emulating their new heroes. The number of international players in the NBA, which was relatively small at the time, began to increase dramatically in the years that followed. Today, the league boasts players from nearly every corner of the globe, a testament to the wide-reaching influence of the Dream Team.

The Dream Team was also instrumental in promoting the NBA brand globally. Their Olympic exploits helped to elevate the league's profile worldwide, leading to increased international television coverage and merchandise sales. The NBA, buoyed by the global popularity of the Dream Team, began to host regular season games in cities outside North America, further expanding its global footprint.

The legacy of the Dream Team is still felt today, more than three decades later. Their impact on the sport of basketball has been profound and lasting. They not only inspired a new generation of players but also changed the way the game is viewed and appreciated around the world. The Dream Team wasn't just a team; it was a phenomenon that transformed basketball forever. Their story is a pivotal chapter in the history of the sport, a story of talent, teamwork, and the power of sport to inspire and unite.

CHAPTER 13:

The Three-Peat Lakers: Shaq, Kobe, and Phil Jackson

In the early 2000s, basketball fans all over the world were treated to a spectacle of skill, teamwork, and tenacity by the Los Angeles Lakers. The team, led by superstar duo Shaquille O'Neal and Kobe Bryant, and guided by the legendary coach Phil Jackson, dominated the NBA, securing three consecutive championships from 2000 to 2002.

The Lakers were already a well-established franchise with a proud history, but the arrival of Jackson, O'Neal, and Bryant took the team to new heights. O'Neal, a powerful and imposing center known for his tremendous size and strength, was an unstoppable force on the court. Bryant, a fiercely competitive shooting guard with an insatiable desire to win, was already showing signs of greatness.

In 1999, Phil Jackson joined the Lakers as their head coach. Jackson, who had previously led the Chicago Bulls to six NBA championships, brought a winning mentality and a unique coaching philosophy to the Lakers. He implemented the "Triangle Offense," a strategic method designed to maximize the skills of the team's best players, and it proved to be a perfect fit for O'Neal and Bryant. With Jackson's guidance, the Lakers' performance steadily improved, and the team was ready to make a run for the championship.

In the 1999-2000 season, the Lakers began their journey toward their first championship in twelve years. O'Neal was named the league's Most Valuable Player (MVP), putting up career-best numbers. Meanwhile, Bryant emerged as one of the league's top scorers and a dominant force in his own right. With Jackson's leadership and the chemistry developing between O'Neal and Bryant, the Lakers finished the regular season with a league-best record of 67 wins and 15 losses.

Their postseason performance was equally impressive. They surged through the playoffs, defeating formidable opponents in the Western Conference. They overcame a challenging series against the Portland Trail Blazers in the Conference Finals, where they staged an unforgettable comeback in Game 7 to secure their spot in the NBA Finals.

They then bested the Indiana Pacers, securing the championship in six games. O'Neal, with his extraordinary Finals performance, earned the Finals MVP honor.

The following year, the Lakers continued their dominance. Despite a somewhat rocky start to the regular season, they hit their stride in the playoffs, sweeping all their opponents in the Western Conference. In the Finals, they faced the Philadelphia 76ers, led by the dynamic Allen Iverson. Despite losing the first game, the Lakers bounced back and won the next four, clinching their second consecutive championship. Again, O'Neal was named Finals MVP.

The Lakers' remarkable run didn't stop there. In the 2001-2002 season, they once again proved their dominance. While facing some stiff competition, they navigated their way to the NBA Finals for a third consecutive year. This time, they faced the New Jersey Nets and swept them in four games. This championship run was particularly special as it marked the first time a team had won three consecutive NBA Championships since the Chicago Bulls did so in the 1990s. O'Neal, once again, was named Finals MVP, capping off an unprecedented and historical run for the Lakers.

This period marked a defining era in Lakers history, with O'Neal, Bryant, and Jackson at the helm. The three-peat accomplishment carved a permanent mark in the NBA's history, further enhancing the legacy of the Lakers' franchise. The combination of O'Neal's dominance, Bryant's skill and determination, and Jackson's unique coaching style created an unforgettable team that basketball fans worldwide still remember fondly today.

While their championship victories were remarkable, the dynamics between Shaquille O'Neal and Kobe Bryant were equally noteworthy. Both players were exceptional talents, but they had distinctly different personalities and approaches to the game. O'Neal was a gregarious and outgoing character who played with a sense of joy and dominance. Bryant, on the other hand, was known for his relentless work ethic, competitive spirit, and determination to win at all costs. This difference in temperament and style created a fascinating dynamic on and off the court.

Despite their contrasting personalities, O'Neal and Bryant complemented each other on the court remarkably well. O'Neal's size, strength, and skills in the paint made him virtually unstoppable close to the basket. Bryant's speed, agility, and scoring prowess from anywhere on the court made him the perfect counterpart. Their distinct yet complementary styles created a potent one-two punch that opponents found hard to counter.

However, their relationship off the court was more complicated. Stories of tension between the two began to surface in the media. There were reports of clashes over leadership roles, differences in work ethic, and disagreements on the court. Despite these challenges, they maintained a professional relationship and continued to perform exceptionally on the court.

In this period, Phil Jackson's role as a coach was pivotal. Known for his Zen-like approach to coaching and his unique ability to manage diverse and strong personalities, Jackson was the perfect figure to guide this Lakers team. He helped the team focus on their collective goal and navigate the complex dynamics to achieve their shared ambition of winning championships.

The Lakers' dominance was not only due to their star players and coach. It was also a testament to the team's depth and the contributions of key role players. Robert Horry, known for his clutch shooting, hit several game-winning shots throughout the team's playoff runs. Derek Fisher provided steady point guard play, while Rick Fox contributed on both ends of the court. Each player had a role to play, and they performed their roles admirably under Jackson's system, further enhancing the team's chemistry and effectiveness.

Off the court, the Lakers were just as captivating as they

were on it. Hollywood celebrities often filled the courtside seats at the Staples Center, and the Lakers were regular features on local and national news. The team's high-profile status, coupled with the drama between O'Neal and Bryant, made them a focal point of attention in the sports world.

The 2001-2002 season marked the end of this era of Lakers dominance. O'Neal was traded to the Miami Heat in 2004, and Jackson temporarily retired from coaching. Despite the breakup of the team, the legacy of the Three-Peat Lakers endures. O'Neal and Bryant are both considered among the greatest players in the history of the sport. Phil Jackson would return to coach the Lakers and lead them to two more championships in 2009 and 2010. Their influence on the game, both in terms of style of play and global popularity, continues to be felt. The Three-Peat Lakers, with their unique blend of talent, personality, and drama, remain one of the most memorable and impactful teams in basketball history.

CHAPTER 14:

Glory Road: The Texas
Western Miners' Historic Win

The year 1966 marked a seismic shift in American college basketball. Against the backdrop of the civil rights movement, a group of young men from Texas Western College (now known as the University of Texas at El Paso) would not only redefine the game but would also challenge societal norms and prejudices. This was the year the Texas Western Miners, led by coach Don Haskins, made history.

The Texas Western Miners had something unique for that time: an all-Black starting lineup. Coach Haskins, known for his disciplined coaching style and tactical acumen, was less concerned with the color of his players' skin and more focused on their talent and ability to contribute to the team. This was a radical departure from the norm, as many teams still adhered to unwritten rules of racial segregation on the court.

The Miners' defining moment came during the NCAA championship game against the University of Kentucky. The Kentucky Wildcats, coached by the legendary Adolph Rupp, were a basketball powerhouse and had an all-white starting lineup. The stark contrast between the two teams was not lost on the audience or the millions watching the game on television.

The game itself was hard-fought, but the Miners' fast-paced style, combined with their tenacious defense, began to take its toll on the Wildcats. As the final buzzer sounded, the Miners emerged victorious with a 72-65 win, making them the first team with an all-black starting lineup to win a national title in U.S. men's college basketball.

The significance of this victory resonated far beyond the hardwood of the basketball court. It was a blow against racial segregation and prejudice. The Miners' victory challenged societal norms and provided a beacon of hope during a tumultuous time in American history. It was a statement that talent and skill know no color.

The impact of this game was profound and lasting. Following this landmark victory, other schools began to recruit Black players more actively. The game also helped to spur the further integration of college sports, breaking down racial barriers and opening the door for a new generation of Black athletes.

The Miners' story inspired the book and subsequent film, 'Glory Road,' which explores themes of racism, discrimination, and student athletics. Their historic season and the legacy they left behind have been honored with induction into the Naismith Memorial Basketball Hall of Fame in 2007. The Texas Western Miners' 1966 championship win remains a pivotal moment in sports history, demonstrating the power of sports to effect change and challenge societal norms.

In the aftermath of the historic win, the Texas Western Miners experienced both praise and backlash. The team's accomplishment was lauded by many as a step forward for civil rights and social change, but it also drew the ire of those resistant to racial integration. The Miners found themselves at the center of a societal issue that extended far beyond the boundaries of a basketball court.

Coach Don Haskins was undeterred by the criticism. His focus had always been on basketball and choosing the best players, regardless of their skin color. The coach's philosophy was simple: "I just played the best players, the ones who could win the game for us." Despite the controversy and the intense pressure, Haskins remained firm in his conviction that he had made the right choices for his team.

The players, too, faced their own set of challenges. Though they were now national champions, they were not immune to the prejudice and discrimination of the era. Some faced hate mail and threats, and they were often met with hostility when they traveled for away games. Yet, they refused to be deterred. They stood tall in the face of adversity, their resolve strengthened by their shared experiences and their groundbreaking accomplishment.

In the end, the 1966 Texas Western Miners team did more than just win a championship. They helped change perceptions, break down barriers, and pave the way for future generations of athletes. Their courage and tenacity in the face of adversity remain inspirational.

The legacy of the 1966 Texas Western Miners is not just in the record books, but in the progress they helped spur in society. Their story is a testament to the power of sports to transcend societal norms and act as a catalyst for change. Today, the Texas Western Miners' story continues to inspire and remind us of the potential for sports to effect significant social change.

The impact of the Miners' triumph reverberated far

beyond the court and the confines of the college basketball world. The victory was a powerful statement in the ongoing battle for civil rights, demonstrating to the nation that talent and skill knew no color. Their victory was symbolic, a beacon of hope and possibility for millions across the nation. They had shattered a ceiling, opening doors for future generations of Black athletes to follow in their footsteps.

In the following years, the number of African American athletes in college sports began to rise. The Miners' victory had laid the groundwork, proving that black athletes could not only compete at the highest level but also win. Teams across the nation began to integrate, realizing that talent was not restricted to one race. The racial makeup of college basketball began to shift, and with it, the nation's perceptions.

The story of the Texas Western Miners was immortalized in the 2006 film 'Glory Road.' The film brought the team's story to a new generation, showcasing their strength, determination, and courage. It served as a reminder of the struggles faced by those who fought against prejudice and discrimination, highlighting the transformative power of sport.

The Texas Western Miners were eventually inducted into the Naismith Memorial Basketball Hall of Fame in 2007, a well-deserved recognition of their pivotal role in the history of basketball. Their story serves as a lasting symbol of the ability of sports to drive societal change and break down barriers. The Miners' win wasn't just a win for the team, it was a win for progress and equality, a shining moment in the fight for civil rights. Their legacy is a timeless reminder of the power of courage, determination, and unity in the face of adversity.

CHAPTER 15:

The Comeback Kids:

Cleveland Cavaliers' Historic

Championship Win

In 2016, the Cleveland Cavaliers achieved what no team had ever done before in the history of the NBA - they won the Championship after being down 3-1 in the Finals. It was a historic comeback, a narrative that would etch the names of LeBron James, Kyrie Irving, and the rest of the Cavaliers into the enduring legacy of the sport.

The stage was set for a clash of titans. The Golden State Warriors, led by the sharpshooting Stephen Curry and versatile Draymond Green, were the defending champions. They had set a record with a remarkable 73-win regular season, surpassing the 1995-96 Chicago Bulls' record. The

Cavaliers, on the other hand, were driven by the desire to bring a championship to the city of Cleveland for the first time in 52 years.

The first four games of the series seemed to affirm the Warriors' dominance. They took a commanding 3-1 lead, and it seemed like the Cavaliers were on the brink of defeat. But LeBron James, the prodigal son who had returned to his hometown team, was not ready to give up. He rallied his team, reminding them that they were not just playing for themselves but for the entire city of Cleveland.

What followed was an incredible display of resilience and tenacity. The Cavaliers won Game 5 on the Warriors' home court, sending a clear message that they were not going down without a fight. Back in Cleveland for Game 6, LeBron James put on a performance for the ages, scoring 41 points to force a decisive Game 7.

Game 7 was a back-and-forth battle, with neither team giving an inch. The turning point came in the final minutes of the game when Kyrie Irving hit a three-pointer to break an 89-89 tie. It was a shot that would go down in history as one of the most clutch in NBA Finals history. LeBron James followed it up with a crucial block on Andre Iguodala, preserving the Cavaliers' lead.

When the final buzzer sounded, the score was 93-89 in favor of the Cavaliers. LeBron James collapsed on the court in tears, the weight of the moment overwhelming him. He had fulfilled his promise - to bring a championship to Cleveland. The city erupted in celebration, their 52-year championship drought finally over. The Cavaliers had achieved the impossible, making a historic comeback and proving to the world that it's never over until it's over.

The aftermath of the 2016 NBA Finals was nothing short of a cultural phenomenon. The city of Cleveland, long deprived of a major sports championship, was ecstatic. Fans poured into the streets to celebrate, tears streaming down their faces, a collective sense of joy, and relief filling the air. The Cavaliers were hailed as heroes, their images adorning murals, billboards, and the front pages of newspapers.

LeBron James, who was unanimously named Finals MVP, was at the center of it all. He averaged a staggering 29.7 points, 11.3 rebounds, 8.9 assists, 2.3 blocks, and 2.6 steals per game in the series, a testament to his all-around brilliance. His legacy, already cemented as one of the greatest basketball players of all time, was further enhanced by the championship win.

The journey of Kyrie Irving was equally noteworthy. His performance in the Finals, particularly his memorable three-pointer in Game 7, established him as one of the game's clutch performers. Irving's shot, a pull-up three over Stephen Curry with less than a minute remaining in a tied Game 7, was as much a testament to his skill and nerve as it was a defining moment in the series. It was a shot that would forever be etched in the minds of basketball fans, symbolic of the Cavaliers' resilience.

But it wasn't just the star players who contributed to the victory. Players like Kevin Love, Tristan Thompson, and J.R. Smith all played crucial roles throughout the series. Love, in particular, had a standout performance in Game 7, grabbing 14 rebounds and playing key defense in the final minutes. Thompson provided critical rebounding and defense throughout the series, while Smith provided timely scoring. Their contributions highlighted the importance of teamwork and collective effort in achieving success.

In the broader context of NBA history, the Cavaliers' championship win was significant for a number of reasons. It marked the first time a team had overcome a 3-1 deficit in the Finals, shattering the notion of an insurmountable lead. It also brought an end to Cleveland's 52-year championship drought, one of the longest in American sports history. Most importantly, it reinforced the belief in the power of resilience and determination, as the Cavaliers, led by LeBron James, defied the odds to claim the ultimate prize in basketball.

The effects of the Cavaliers' historic win resonated far beyond the basketball court. The championship was a boon for the city of Cleveland, injecting a new sense of vitality and pride into a city that had often been overlooked. The Cavaliers' triumph had a powerful, uplifting effect on the city's residents, providing them with a source of joy and pride that transcended sports. In many ways, the Cavaliers' victory was symbolic of the city's resilience and tenacity, characteristics that have defined Cleveland and its people.

In the world of basketball, the Cavaliers' win marked a shift in the power dynamics of the NBA. The Golden State Warriors, who had been near-invincible throughout the 2015-16 season, were suddenly human, their aura of invincibility shattered. The Cavaliers' victory served as a reminder of the unpredictable nature of sports and the fact that no lead, no matter how commanding, is safe.

For LeBron James, the win solidified his status as one of the greatest basketball players of all time. Having brought a championship to his hometown team, against all odds, James had fulfilled his promise and cemented his legacy. The victory also boosted his standing in the perennial debate over the greatest basketball player of all time, a discussion that often centers around James and Michael Jordan.

In the end, the story of the 2016 Cleveland Cavaliers is one of determination, resilience, and a never-give-up attitude. It's a story that transcends basketball and touches on broader themes of perseverance, unity, and the power of belief. It's a story that will be remembered, cherished, and recounted in the world of sports for generations to come. The tale of the Cavaliers' historic comeback serves as an enduring testament to the magic of sports and the unyielding spirit of competition.

CHAPTER 16:

Giannis Antetokounmpo:
From Street Vendor to NBA MVP

The NBA has a rich history of players who have overcome adversity to achieve greatness, but few stories are as compelling as that of Giannis Antetokounmpo. Born in Athens, Greece, to Nigerian immigrants, Antetokounmpo's journey from humble beginnings to the apex of the basketball world is a testament to his unwavering determination, tenacity, and relentless work ethic.

Giannis and his family faced significant hardship in their early years in Greece. As undocumented immigrants, they lived in poverty, and Giannis and his older brother, Thanasis, often had to work as street vendors to help support their family. They would sell items such as watches, bags, and sunglasses, earning just enough to get by. Despite these hardships, Giannis found solace in basketball, a sport he came to love after being introduced to it by his older brother.

His raw talent was evident from an early age. Standing at an impressive height and possessing natural athletic ability, Giannis quickly made a name for himself in local leagues. Despite his lack of formal training and resources, his passion for the game shone through. He would often play in old, worn-out shoes and share a pair with his brother due to their limited means.

In 2012, at the age of 17, Antetokounmpo began playing for Filathlitikos in Greece's second-tier basketball league. His performances caught the attention of NBA scouts, and in 2013, he declared for the NBA draft. The Milwaukee Bucks selected him with the 15th overall pick, a decision that would change the course of the franchise.

In the NBA, Giannis continued to impress with his unique blend of size, speed, and skill. His ability to play and defend multiple positions, coupled with his relentless drive, quickly made him one of the league's most exciting players. His breakout season came in 2016-17, when he was named the NBA's Most Improved Player. However, it was just the beginning for the young Greek phenom.

In the following years, Antetokounmpo ascended to the top echelon of the NBA, earning back-to-back MVP awards in 2019 and 2020. His rise to superstardom, from a street vendor in Athens to one of the most dominant players in the NBA, is a powerful reminder of the transformative potential of sports.

Giannis Antetokounmpo's story is one of perseverance, determination, and an unwavering belief in oneself. It is a story that transcends basketball and serves as an inspiration to countless individuals around the world. The "Greek Freak," as he is affectionately known, has carved out his place in NBA history, and his journey from the streets of Athens to NBA MVP stands as one of the most remarkable in the sport's history.

Building on his personal success, Giannis Antetokounmpo has also become a beacon for international players seeking to make their mark in the NBA. His rise to stardom has opened doors for many young players from around the world, and his influence extends far beyond the court.

Antetokounmpo's impact on the game of basketball in Greece has been profound. His success has sparked a surge of interest in the sport, with more and more young people taking up basketball. He has become a national hero in his home country, with his games often broadcast on national television and his performances closely followed by Greek fans.

In addition to his on-court exploits, Giannis is also renowned for his humility and his commitment to his family. Despite his fame and fortune, he has remained grounded, often speaking about the importance of his family in his life. He has used his platform to shed light on issues close to his heart, including immigration and poverty.

But perhaps the most significant aspect of Giannis Antetokounmpo's story is the hope it instills. It is a shining example of how far hard work, dedication, and a dream can take you. It is a testament to the notion that no matter where you come from, no matter your circumstances, you can achieve greatness if you believe in yourself and never give up.

As Giannis Antetokounmpo's career continues to unfold, his impact on the game, both on and off the court, is undeniable. His style of play, combining agility, speed, and power, has redefined the possibilities for a player of his size. His unique blend of skills and size, often referred to as positionless basketball, has been a game-changer, forcing teams to rethink their strategies and player development.

The Antetokounmpo effect is not just limited to his own team, the Milwaukee Bucks, but has rippled through the entire

NBA. His ability to play and guard multiple positions has placed a premium on versatility in the league. This has led to a shift in player evaluation, with teams now seeking players who possess a diverse range of skills, rather than traditional, position-specific abilities.

Off the court, Giannis has leveraged his success to make a difference. He is involved in numerous charitable activities, including efforts to combat childhood hunger and improve education. He has also established the "Antetokounbros Academy," a program aimed at developing young Greek athletes. His philanthropic efforts have earned him much admiration and further solidified his status as a role model.

In the realm of business and marketing, Giannis has also made significant strides. He has signed endorsement deals with several major companies, including Nike, and even has his own signature shoe. His marketability continues to rise along with his on-court success, making him one of the most recognizable faces in the sport.

As Giannis Antetokounmpo continues to carve out his legacy in the NBA, his story serves as a powerful reminder of the transformative power of sports. From a young boy selling goods on the streets of Athens to a two-time NBA MVP, his journey is a testament to the human spirit's resilience and the endless possibilities that come with determination and hard work. His story continues to inspire millions around the world, showing that no obstacle is too great to overcome in the pursuit of a dream.

CHAPTER 17:

The Chicago Bulls: The Dynasty of the

90s

In the history of the NBA, few teams have captured the public's imagination quite like the Chicago Bulls of the 1990s. Under the leadership of Head Coach Phil Jackson, and with the extraordinary talent of players like Michael Jordan, Scottie Pippen, and Dennis Rodman, the Bulls dominated the NBA landscape, securing six championships in a span of eight years and setting a new standard for excellence in professional basketball.

In the early 90s, the Bulls emerged as a powerhouse, with Michael Jordan's meteoric rise to superstardom catalyzing the team's ascension. After years of coming up short against rivals like the Detroit Pistons, the Bulls finally broke through in the

1990-1991 season, defeating the Los Angeles Lakers to win their first championship.

The following two seasons saw the Bulls establish their dominance, winning back-to-back championships and cementing their place in NBA lore. The team's success was not solely due to their talent, but also to their unselfish style of play, popularized by Phil Jackson's implementation of the triangle offense, and their relentless defense.

After a brief retirement, Jordan returned to the Bulls in 1995, setting the stage for a second three-peat. Joined by Pippen and the enigmatic Rodman, the Bulls embarked on one of the most impressive runs in NBA history, winning three more championships from 1996 to 1998.

The 1995-1996 season was particularly memorable, as the Bulls set an NBA record with 72 regular season wins, a record that stood for two decades. That season culminated in the Bulls winning their fourth championship, with Jordan being named the Finals MVP.

However, the success of the Bulls was not without its trials and tribulations. Tensions within the team and with management, particularly General Manager Jerry Krause, led to the eventual dissolution of the dynasty. After winning their sixth championship in 1998, Phil Jackson left the Bulls, followed by the departures of Jordan and Pippen.

Despite the tumultuous end, the legacy of the 90s Bulls remains intact. They are often regarded as one of the greatest teams in the history of sports, with their influence extending well beyond the basketball court. The team's popularity globally helped propel the NBA to new heights of international visibility and commercial success. Even today, the 90s Bulls are synonymous with basketball excellence, their impact etched into the fabric of the sport.

As dominant as the Bulls were on the court, their impact off the court was just as significant. They were cultural icons, transforming the NBA from a largely American sport into a global phenomenon. The team's appeal transcended national borders, attracting fans from all corners of the world.

Michael Jordan, the lynchpin of the Bulls' success, was at the center of this cultural shift. With his extraordinary athleticism, competitive fire, and larger-than-life persona, Jordan became a global icon. His influence reached far beyond the hardwood, shaping fashion trends with his signature line of Nike sneakers, and even starring in the hit film "Space Jam". His charisma and on-court brilliance made him one of the most recognizable figures in the world, and he used this platform to promote the sport on an international scale.

Scottie Pippen, Jordan's trusted sidekick, was equally instrumental in the Bulls' success. An exceptional all-around player, Pippen's versatility on both ends of the floor made him the perfect complement to Jordan. He often took on the task of guarding the opposing team's best player, and his ability to facilitate the offense made him an invaluable component of the Bulls' system. Pippen's contributions often flew under the radar due to Jordan's overwhelming presence, but his importance to the team's success cannot be overstated.

Then there was Dennis Rodman, the team's wild card. Known for his colorful hair, numerous tattoos, and unpredictable behavior off the court, Rodman was a spectacle in his own right. However, on the court, he was a relentless rebounder and a tenacious defender, adding a gritty edge to the Bulls' star-studded roster. Rodman's eccentric personality added another layer of intrigue to the team, further amplifying the Bulls' appeal.

This trio, along with a strong supporting cast featuring players like Toni Kukoč and Steve Kerr, made the Bulls an unstoppable force. The team's style, personality, and dominance captivated audiences, making every Bulls game a must-watch event.

The Bulls' influence is still felt in the NBA today. They set the blueprint for constructing a championship team, demonstrating the importance of not only assembling talented players, but also cultivating an unselfish culture and a strong defensive mentality. The lessons from the Bulls' dynasty continue to inform team-building strategies in the modern NBA, a testament to their lasting impact on the sport.

The Bulls' dominance in the 90s was also guided by the strategic mastermind, Phil Jackson. As head coach, Jackson was the orchestrator of the Bulls' symphony, managing a multitude of strong personalities and ensuring they all functioned harmoniously on the court. Jackson, who had already won a championship as a player with the New York Knicks, brought a unique perspective to his coaching philosophy, incorporating elements of Zen Buddhism and Native American spirituality into his approach.

Perhaps Jackson's most significant contribution was implementing the triangle offense, a system that emphasizes spacing, passing, and constant motion. The triangle offense was a departure from the isolation-heavy strategies common in the NBA at the time. By creating more opportunities for team play and fluid ball movement, Jackson was able to maximize the unique talents of his players while promoting a team-first mentality.

Michael Jordan, a dominant scorer, thrived in this system, which allowed him to exploit defensive weaknesses while also creating opportunities for his teammates. Scottie Pippen's versatility was also highlighted, with the offense often running through him due to his exceptional passing and playmaking abilities. Even Dennis Rodman, known more for his defense and rebounding, found his niche within the system, often initiating the offense with his ability to secure offensive rebounds.

However, the implementation of the triangle offense was not without its challenges. Jackson faced initial resistance, especially from Jordan, who was accustomed to having the ball in his hands and dictating the pace of the game. But Jackson's unwavering commitment to the system, along with his ability to communicate its benefits to his players, eventually won over the team. The success that followed served as a validation of Jackson's innovative approach.

Under Phil Jackson's leadership, the Chicago Bulls transcended the realm of sports to become a cultural phenomenon. Their impact extended beyond the borders of the United States, ushering in a new era of global popularity for the NBA. The Bulls' dynasty of the 90s remains one of the most memorable periods in basketball history, with their influence still evident in today's game.

In the midst of the Chicago Bulls' reign, a key piece of their success was the indomitable Scottie Pippen. Often described as the perfect counterpart to Jordan, Pippen was the glue that held the team together. His versatile skill set allowed him to impact the game in a multitude of ways - from scoring and playmaking to defense and leadership. Pippen's contributions often flew under the radar due to the colossal shadow cast by Jordan, but his value to the team was immeasurable.

Pippen's ability to guard multiple positions with his length, quickness, and defensive intelligence was a significant asset for the Bulls. He was regularly tasked with guarding the opposing team's best player, freeing up Jordan to focus more on the offensive end of the court. Moreover, Pippen's understanding of team defense, coupled with his excellent communication skills, made him the defensive anchor of the Bulls.

Offensively, Pippen was a Swiss army knife. He could score at the rim, from mid-range, or beyond the three-point line, but his most significant contribution came in the form of playmaking. With his vision and basketball IQ, Pippen often acted as a point forward, initiating the offense and creating opportunities for his teammates. His unselfishness and ability to read the game were key factors in the successful implementation of the triangle offense.

Beyond his on-court contributions, Pippen's role as a

leader was pivotal. He served as a buffer between the hard-driving Jordan and the rest of the team, often providing a calming influence in high-pressure situations. His steady demeanor and approachability played a crucial role in maintaining team chemistry during their intense championship runs.

Towards the end of the 90s, as age and fatigue began to set in, the Bulls' dominance started to wane. The team was embroiled in internal conflict, particularly between General Manager Jerry Krause and key members of the team and coaching staff. Despite the turmoil, the Bulls managed to secure their second three-peat with a thrilling victory over the Utah Jazz in the 1998 NBA Finals, a testament to their resilience and winning mentality.

The 1997-98 season marked the end of the Bulls' dynasty. Phil Jackson left the team, and Michael Jordan announced his second retirement. Pippen was traded to the Houston Rockets, and Rodman was released. The team entered a rebuilding phase that would last for several years.

Despite their eventual breakup, the Chicago Bulls of the 90s left an enduring legacy. They were a team that not only won but did so with a style and swagger that captured the imagination of fans worldwide. Their influence on the game of basketball is undeniable, and their story remains a quintessential part of the NBA's rich history.

CHAPTER 18:

The Story of Kareem Abdul-Jabbar: The NBA's All-Time Leading Scorer

Kareem Abdul-Jabbar's journey from a young boy in New York City to the NBA's all-time leading scorer is a story of talent, perseverance, and the refinement of one of basketball's most iconic weapons—the skyhook.

Born Ferdinand Lewis Alcindor Jr., Kareem Abdul-Jabbar was introduced to the game of basketball at a young age. His talent was evident early on, and he was a standout player at Power Memorial High School in New York City, where he led his team to three straight New York City Catholic championships, compiling a remarkable 71-game winning streak and a 79-2 overall record.

His dominance continued in college, where he played for

the UCLA Bruins under the legendary coach John Wooden. During his time at UCLA, Abdul-Jabbar led the Bruins to three NCAA championships and was a three-time Most Outstanding Player in the NCAA Tournament—a feat that has not been matched since. His success at the collegiate level led to his selection as the first overall pick in the 1969 NBA draft by the Milwaukee Bucks.

In his first season with the Bucks, Abdul-Jabbar, still known by his birth name of Alcindor, was named NBA Rookie of the Year. In his second season, he led the Bucks to their first and, to date, only NBA championship, earning the Finals MVP in the process. It was during his time in Milwaukee that he converted to Islam and changed his name to Kareem Abdul-Jabbar, which means "noble, powerful servant."

In 1975, Abdul-Jabbar was traded to the Los Angeles Lakers, where he would go on to form one of the most successful partnerships in NBA history with Magic Johnson. The duo, known for their "Showtime" style of play, led the Lakers to five NBA championships during the 1980s. Despite his advancing age, Abdul-Jabbar's production remained consistent, and in 1984, he surpassed Wilt Chamberlain as the NBA's all-time leading scorer—a record he still holds today.

Throughout his career, Abdul-Jabbar was recognized not

just for his scoring ability, but also for his defensive prowess. He was an 11-time All-Defensive Team selection and a record six-time NBA MVP. But it was his skyhook shot that left an indelible mark on the game. A graceful, almost unblockable shot, the skyhook became Abdul-Jabbar's signature move and contributed significantly to his scoring record.

Abdul-Jabbar retired in 1989 after 20 seasons in the NBA. His number 33 jersey has been retired by both the Bucks and the Lakers, and in 1995, he was inducted into the Naismith Memorial Basketball Hall of Fame. But his impact extends beyond the basketball court. As an author, activist, and cultural ambassador, Abdul-Jabbar has continued to make significant contributions to society, using his platform to advocate for social justice and education.

The story of Kareem Abdul-Jabbar is more than just basketball. It's a story of a man who, through his talent and determination, not only reached the pinnacle of his sport but also used his position to impact the world around him. Today, his name stands atop the list of NBA's all-time leading scorers, a testament to his remarkable career and enduring legacy.

It is important to understand the impact of his skyhook shot on the game of basketball. The skyhook, a one-handed shot where the shooter extends his arm and flicks his wrist to send the ball towards the hoop in an arching motion, was not an invention of Abdul-Jabbar's, but he was the player who made it famous. With his 7-foot-2 height and incredible skill, Abdul-Jabbar's skyhook was virtually unblockable and became one of the most effective offensive weapons in the history of the sport.

Abdul-Jabbar's skyhook was a result of years of practice and refinement. As a child, he had been taught the shot by his coach and mentor, Jack Donahue, as a way to take advantage of his height. Abdul-Jabbar perfected the shot over the years, using it to devastating effect throughout his collegiate and professional career. It became his signature move, a symbol of his dominance on the basketball court.

Off the court, Abdul-Jabbar was just as impactful. He was an outspoken advocate for social justice, using his platform to address issues of race and inequality. After his retirement, he continued to be a voice for change, writing books and articles on a range of social and political issues. His activism and commitment to change earned him the Presidential Medal of Freedom in 2016, the highest civilian award in the United States.

Abdul-Jabbar's influence also extended to future generations of players. His scoring record, the effectiveness of his skyhook, and his success on the court set a benchmark for future athletes. Players like Magic Johnson, Shaquille O'Neal, and LeBron James have all spoken about the impact of Abdul-Jabbar's game on their own careers. His skyhook shot, while not widely used in today's game, is still considered one of the most iconic shots in basketball history.

Kareem Abdul-Jabbar's story is one of a relentless pursuit of excellence, both on and off the court. His journey from a child playing basketball in New York City to becoming the NBA's all-time leading scorer is a testament to his hard work, dedication, and immense talent. His impact on the game of basketball, his advocacy for social justice, and his influence on future generations make him a true legend of the sport.

As we continue to explore the journey of Kareem Abdul-Jabbar, we must also focus on his years with the Los Angeles Lakers, where he formed an iconic duo with Magic Johnson and won five of his six NBA championships. Traded to the Lakers in 1975, Abdul-Jabbar was initially apprehensive about the move. However, he soon found a new home in Los Angeles, both on and off the court.

The arrival of Earvin "Magic" Johnson in the 1979 NBA draft marked a turning point in Abdul-Jabbar's career. The young point guard's charismatic personality and flashy style of play complemented Abdul-Jabbar's quiet demeanor and methodical approach to the game. Together, they formed the backbone of the Lakers' "Showtime" era, a period of fast-paced, high-scoring basketball that captivated fans across the nation.

Magic Johnson's court vision and passing ability combined perfectly with Abdul-Jabbar's scoring prowess. Johnson would often deliver no-look passes to Abdul-Jabbar, who would then finish with his patented skyhook. Their partnership was a key factor in the Lakers' dominance during the 1980s, leading the team to five championships in a nine-year span.

Off the court, Abdul-Jabbar was a prominent figure in the Los Angeles community. He was known for his intellectual pursuits, with interests in history, philosophy, and martial arts. He also started his writing career during his time with the Lakers, publishing several books on a variety of topics.

After his retirement in 1989, Abdul-Jabbar remained involved in basketball, serving as a special assistant coach for the Lakers and other teams. He has also been a mentor to many younger players, sharing his knowledge and experience with the next generation.

Kareem Abdul-Jabbar's time with the Los Angeles Lakers was marked by success, partnership, and community involvement. His on-court partnership with Magic Johnson created one of the most successful eras in Lakers history, while his off-court pursuits demonstrated his broad interests and commitment to his community. His influence extends far beyond his playing career, as he continues to impact the game of basketball and society at large.

Last, we cannot discuss Kareem Abdul-Jabbar's story without acknowledging his advocacy for social justice and his role as a cultural ambassador. He has consistently used his platform to address various societal issues, making significant contributions off the court that are just as impactful as his on-court achievements.

Throughout his career and into his retirement, Abdul-Jabbar has been a vocal advocate for racial and social justice. He has written and spoken extensively on these topics, using his platform to promote change and challenge inequality. His commitment to activism was evident even during his playing days, when he famously boycotted the 1968 Olympics in protest of racial inequality in the United States.

In his post-basketball career, Abdul-Jabbar has also served as a cultural ambassador for the United States. In 2012, he was appointed as a U.S. global cultural ambassador by then-Secretary of State Hillary Clinton. In this role, he has traveled the world to engage in dialogue on behalf of the United States, promoting cultural understanding and mutual respect.

Abdul-Jabbar's influence extends to his work in education as well. In 2015, he launched the Skyhook Foundation, an organization aimed at giving kids a "shot that can't be blocked" by bringing educational STEM opportunities to underserved communities. Through this initiative, Abdul-Jabbar continues to make a positive impact on the lives of young people, demonstrating his dedication to empowering future generations.

Kareem Abdul-Jabbar's legacy is marked by excellence, persistence, and a deep commitment to social justice. His journey from the playgrounds of New York to becoming the all-time leading scorer in NBA history is a testament to his remarkable talent and determination. But perhaps more importantly, his contributions off the court—as an advocate, an ambassador, and an educator—have cemented his status as a true icon, not just in the realm of sports, but in the broader cultural landscape as well. His story serves as an inspiring example of the power of sports to transcend boundaries and effect positive change.

CHAPTER 19:

The Redeem Team: A 2008 Olympics Redemption Story

After the disappointment of the 2004 Olympics, when the U.S. men's basketball team failed to secure the gold medal, American basketball was in a period of reflection and soul-searching. The world had caught up, and the days of simply sending twelve NBA players to the Games and expecting them to return with gold were over. The United States needed a team, not just a collection of stars, to regain the top spot on the global stage. Thus, the stage was set for the 2008 Olympics in Beijing, China, and the formation of the U.S. team that would come to be known as the "Redeem Team."

The Redeem Team was a carefully selected group of

NBA stars who were not only exceptional players but also understood the importance of team play and were willing to put the team's success above their individual achievements. The roster was stacked with talent, featuring the likes of Kobe Bryant, LeBron James, Dwyane Wade, and Carmelo Anthony. But perhaps the most critical element of the team's formation was the appointment of Duke University's legendary coach, Mike Krzyzewski, as head coach, with a supporting cast of experienced NBA coaches including Jim Boeheim, Mike D'Antoni, and Nate McMillan.

Coach Krzyzewski, or Coach K as he's often called, had a reputation for developing a strong team culture, emphasizing the importance of teamwork, discipline, and hard work. He drilled into the players that no one was bigger than the team and that they would have to play together if they wanted to regain the gold.

The Redeem Team lived up to its name in Beijing, demonstrating a renewed commitment to team play and dominant performances that silenced critics. They stormed through the preliminary round with a perfect record, winning by an average margin of over 30 points. The quarterfinal and semifinal games proved more challenging, but the team's cohesion and determination saw them through.

In the gold medal game, the U.S. faced Spain, a team

boasting its own NBA talent, including Pau Gasol and Rudy Fernandez. In a thrilling match, the Redeem Team showed their mettle. With the Spaniards mounting a tough challenge, Kobe Bryant and Dwyane Wade stepped up, making key plays in the final minutes to seal the victory for the United States. The final buzzer sounded with the scoreboard reading 118-107 in favor of the U.S., marking the return of American basketball to Olympic glory.

The Redeem Team had achieved their mission. They had not only won the gold medal but had done so by playing as a team, demonstrating the best of American basketball. The Redeem Team's journey to gold was a redemption story for American basketball and a testament to the power of teamwork, discipline, and a shared commitment to a common goal. The legacy of the 2008 Redeem Team continues to influence the way U.S. Olympic basketball teams are assembled and how they approach international competition.

The Redeem Team's success was not just about the games they won; it was about the change they brought to the perception of American basketball on the international stage. The 2004 team's failure was seen by many as an indication of American arrogance, a belief that individual talent alone was enough to conquer the world. But the 2008 team showed that the U.S. understood the importance of team play, of sacrificing personal glory for collective success, and of giving due respect to international competition.

The players themselves underwent a transformation. They came into the Olympic training camp as NBA stars, each accustomed to being the focal point of their respective teams. However, under the guidance of Coach K, they quickly learned to put aside their egos and play for each other. The camaraderie and respect they developed for one another was evident in the way they played on the court. They shared the ball, they defended as a unit, and when one of them was in trouble, others stepped up.

Perhaps the best example of this team spirit came in the form of Kobe Bryant, the NBA's reigning MVP at the time. Known for his fierce competitiveness and scoring prowess, Bryant took on the role of the team's defensive stopper, often guarding the opponent's best player. He accepted this role willingly, understanding that his sacrifice was necessary for the team's success. His commitment to the team embodied the spirit of the Redeem Team.

Off the court, the players were ambassadors, representing their country with grace and humility. They interacted with athletes from other sports, attended their games, and showed appreciation for their talent and efforts. Their behavior won them fans not just in America but around the world, helping to restore the image of American basketball.

The impact of the Redeem Team's journey extends beyond the players and coaches involved. It served as a blueprint for building successful international teams - a combination of talent, teamwork, coaching, and respect for the competition. It also inspired a generation of young players, showing them that even at the highest level of the sport, teamwork is paramount.

As the final notes of the American national anthem rang out in the Beijing Olympic Basketball Gymnasium, and the gold medals hung around the players' necks, it was clear that the Redeem Team had achieved more than just a win. They had sparked a change in American basketball, and their story continues to resonate, a symbol of redemption, unity, and the true spirit of the sport.

The aftermath of the 2008 Olympics saw the Redeem Team players return to their respective NBA franchises as changed athletes. Their summer together in Beijing had taught them about sacrifice, respect, and the value of teamwork. These lessons did not just stay on the Olympic court; they transformed the players' approach to the game and had a profound impact on their NBA careers.

LeBron James, already a dominant player in the league,

emerged as an even better leader, showing a newfound commitment to defense and team play. His improved all-around game helped the Miami Heat win two NBA championships. Kobe Bryant, too, applied the lessons from his Olympic experience to his play in the NBA, leading the Los Angeles Lakers to two more championships in 2009 and 2010.

Similarly, other members of the team, including Dwyane Wade, Chris Bosh, and Carmelo Anthony, enjoyed successful post-Olympic careers, their games enriched by the experience of playing for the Redeem Team. They understood that while individual accolades were important, the success of the team was paramount.

But perhaps the most important legacy of the Redeem Team was the change it brought about in the USA Basketball program. Jerry Colangelo and Coach K had successfully rebuilt the program by instilling a culture of respect, commitment, and teamwork. Their approach became a model for future teams.

In the following Olympics in 2012 and 2016, the U.S. men's basketball teams continued the Redeem Team's legacy, winning gold medals and dominating the international stage. The players on these teams, many of whom grew up watching the Redeem Team's heroics in 2008, carried forward the same values of team play and respect for international competition.

The story of the Redeem Team is thus not just about a single tournament or a gold medal win. It is about the transformation of American basketball, the redemption of its global image, and the creation of a legacy that continues to inspire future generations. The Redeem Team will always be remembered as the team that brought back the glory days of American basketball and set a new standard for what it means to represent one's country on the international stage.

Even as the legacy of the Redeem Team unfolded on the court, its influence stretched far beyond the arenas and TV screens. The team's story became a symbol of resilience and redemption, an inspiring tale that transcended sports. It reminded people that failure, while painful, could be a stepping stone to success if met with determination and a willingness to learn and grow.

The story of the Redeem Team also underscored the importance of humility. The 2004 team, despite its star-studded roster, had failed to respect their opponents and the game. They learned the hard way that talent alone could not guarantee victory. In contrast, the 2008 team, despite being equally talented, approached their task with humility and respect. They understood that winning required more than just individual brilliance - it needed teamwork, dedication, and a deep respect for the game and the competition.

Moreover, the Redeem Team's journey illustrated the power of unity. The team was composed of fierce competitors who were used to battling each other in the NBA. Yet, they came together as one, setting aside their egos and personal agendas for a common goal. They were united not just by their shared love for the game, but also by a shared purpose: to restore their nation's pride in basketball.

The players' commitment to their country also shone through. Many of them had to forgo personal interests and make sacrifices to be a part of the Olympic team. Their decision to represent their country on the world stage, despite the challenges, was a testament to their patriotism and love for the sport.

The Redeem Team's story continues to inspire athletes and non-athletes alike. It is a reminder that with humility, unity, respect, and determination, it is possible to overcome even the most daunting challenges and achieve greatness. The story of the Redeem Team is a testament to the power of redemption, and it remains an important chapter in the history of American basketball.

CHAPTER 20:

The Showtime Era: Magic Johnson and the Los Angeles Lakers

In the history of basketball, few eras are as emblematic of a team's culture and style as the "Showtime" era of the Los Angeles Lakers. This period, spanning the 1980s, was marked by a fast-paced, flamboyant style of play that not only brought consistent success to the Lakers but also revolutionized the way basketball was played and viewed.

At the heart of Showtime was Earvin "Magic" Johnson, the charismatic point guard whose dazzling playmaking and infectious smile became the face of the Lakers and the NBA. Drafted first overall by the Lakers in 1979, Magic quickly made a name for himself with his remarkable court vision, passing skills, and ability to make his teammates better. At

6'9", he was a point guard in a power forward's body, a unique attribute that allowed him to dominate games in ways few others could.

Magic's arrival in Los Angeles coincided with the Lakers' acquisition of several key players that would become integral to the Showtime era. This included the likes of James Worthy, Byron Scott, Michael Cooper, and, of course, Kareem Abdul-Jabbar, the NBA's all-time leading scorer. Under the guidance of head coach Pat Riley, these players developed a chemistry and style of play that was tailor-made for the Hollywood setting they represented.

Showtime was about more than just basketball, though. It was an entertainment spectacle that perfectly encapsulated the glitz and glamour of Los Angeles. The fast-break offense, the no-look passes, the slam dunks - every Lakers game was an event, a must-see show. This was reflected in the star-studded crowds that regularly filled the Forum, the Lakers' home court. Celebrities like Jack Nicholson and Diane Cannon were regular attendees, their presence adding to the aura of Showtime.

On the court, the results were undeniable. The Lakers won five NBA championships during the Showtime era (1980, 1982, 1985, 1987, and 1988), with Magic Johnson winning three Most Valuable Player (MVP) Awards (1987, 1989, and

1990). The team's success was a testament to their skill, but also to their ability to perform under pressure. In the bright lights and big moments, the Showtime Lakers always seemed to deliver.

The Showtime era left an enduring legacy on the NBA. It popularized a style of play that prioritized speed, creativity, and excitement. It set a new standard for what a basketball team could be, both on and off the court. And it provided some of the most memorable moments and iconic players in the history of the sport.

But perhaps the most significant legacy of Showtime is the influence it had on future generations of players. Today, you can see traces of Showtime in the up-tempo, high-scoring style of play that many teams favor. The era's emphasis on showmanship and entertainment is also reflected in the NBA's global popularity and its place in pop culture.

Above all, the Showtime era encapsulated the joy of basketball. It was a period defined by a love for the game, a love that was reflected in the way the Lakers played and in the way fans around the world responded. It was, in every sense, a magical time in the history of the NBA.

The Showtime Lakers weren't just about the stars on the court, they were also about the man on the sidelines – Pat

Riley. With his slicked-back hair and Armani suits, Riley was as much a part of the Showtime image as Magic Johnson's no-look passes or Kareem Abdul-Jabbar's skyhooks. He brought a level of professionalism and intensity to the team that helped elevate them to greatness.

Riley understood the unique blend of talent he had at his disposal and designed an offensive scheme that fully capitalized on it. The Lakers played a fast-paced, free-flowing style of basketball that was a joy to watch and a nightmare for opposing teams to defend. They constantly pushed the pace, looking to score easy baskets on the fast break before the defense could get set.

The offensive genius of the Showtime Lakers was matched by their commitment to defense. Under Riley's tutelage, the Lakers became one of the best defensive teams in the league. They used their athleticism and length to disrupt opponents, creating turnovers that often led to fast break opportunities.

One of the key components of the Showtime Lakers was their depth. Beyond the headline stars, players like Kurt Rambis, A.C. Green, and Mychal Thompson played crucial roles. They provided energy, toughness, and solid play off the bench, allowing the Lakers to maintain their frenetic pace for the full 48 minutes.

The rivalry with the Boston Celtics during this period also added to the Showtime Lakers' story. These two storied franchises clashed multiple times in the NBA Finals during the 1980s, with the likes of Larry Bird, Robert Parish, and Kevin McHale going toe-to-toe with the Lakers. These epic battles, full of memorable moments and high drama, brought even more attention and acclaim to the Showtime Lakers.

However, the Showtime era wasn't without its challenges. Injuries, especially Magic Johnson's knee issues, tested the team's resilience. Magic's shocking announcement in 1991 that he had contracted HIV, effectively ended the Showtime era. His subsequent retirement was a significant blow to the Lakers and the entire sports world.

Despite these challenges, the Showtime Lakers left an indelible mark on the sport. Their style of play, their success, and their cultural impact continue to resonate. They entertained millions and, in doing so, shaped the future of the NBA. The Showtime Lakers were not just a team; they were an experience, an embodiment of the magic of basketball.

The Showtime Lakers were not just defined by their style of play on the court, but also by the era and location in which they thrived. Los Angeles in the 1980s was a city buzzing with glitz, glamour, and celebrity, and the Lakers were the heartbeat of it all. The team's fast-paced, electrifying style of play matched the city's vibrant energy, and the stars of Hollywood were drawn to the spectacle.

Laker games at the Forum in Inglewood were must-attend events, attracting a who's who of Hollywood. Movie stars, musicians, and celebrities from all walks of life flocked to the arena to watch Magic, Kareem, and the rest of the Lakers dazzle on the court. The courtside seats were often filled with famous faces, and the atmosphere was electric. The team's success on the court and the exciting brand of basketball they played made them a part of the city's cultural fabric.

The Showtime era wasn't just about winning games and championships; it was about doing so with flair and style. The team's charismatic leader, Magic Johnson, embodied this spirit. With his infectious smile, flashy passes, and clutch performances, Magic became an icon not just in Los Angeles, but across the globe. His rivalry and friendship with Larry Bird, which started in college and continued into the pros, added an extra layer of intrigue and excitement to the NBA.

Kareem Abdul-Jabbar's contributions to the Showtime Lakers should also not be overlooked. The six-time MVP and all-time leading scorer in NBA history provided the team with a reliable scoring option and a defensive anchor. His skyhook shot became one of the most iconic and unguardable moves in basketball history.

The Showtime Lakers also benefited from a strong supporting cast. James Worthy, a seven-time All-Star and Finals MVP, was a versatile scorer and a key player in the Lakers' success. Byron Scott provided reliable outside shooting, while Michael Cooper was a defensive stalwart and the 1987 Defensive Player of the Year.

The Showtime era came to an end with Magic Johnson's early retirement in 1991, but its impact on the Lakers franchise and the NBA as a whole is undeniable. The team's success during this period cemented the Lakers as one of the premier franchises in the NBA. Their fast-paced, entertaining style of play influenced future generations of teams and helped popularize the NBA worldwide. The Showtime Lakers were more than just a basketball team; they were a cultural phenomenon that transcended the sport.

Even though the Showtime era was defined by its fast-break basketball and flashy style, it was the Lakers' commitment to teamwork and strategic basketball that truly set them apart. The man at the helm during this period, coach Pat Riley, was instrumental in creating this culture.

Riley, a former player himself, understood the nuances of the game and the personalities of his players. He knew how to extract the best from his team, pushing them to their limits while also building a strong camaraderie. Riley's approach was intense and demanding, but he also fostered an environment where players felt valued and understood. His coaching philosophy was built around the idea of "the innocent climb," a belief in the power of unity, selflessness, and relentless effort.

Under Riley, the Lakers implemented a fast-paced offense that took full advantage of Magic's superb court vision and playmaking abilities. The offense was designed to push the pace and create scoring opportunities before the defense could get set. But the Lakers were not just an offensive powerhouse; they were also strong defensively. Michael Cooper was the team's defensive ace, often tasked with guarding the opponent's best player. The Lakers' defense was just as integral to their success as their celebrated offense.

As a testament to Riley's coaching acumen, the Lakers reached the NBA Finals in each of his first four seasons as head coach, winning two championships in the process. He would go on to win two more titles with the Lakers in 1987 and 1988, cementing the team's status as a dynasty.

The Showtime Lakers were a team for the ages, leaving a lasting imprint on the NBA. They were a team that perfectly captured the spirit of their time and place, a team that brought glamour and excitement to the game of basketball. Their legacy goes beyond the five championships they won or the numerous records they set. The Showtime Lakers revolutionized the game with their style of play, set a new standard for team basketball, and captured the hearts of fans all over the world.

As we turn the final page on the Showtime era, we remember not just the victories and the championships, but the joy and excitement that the Lakers brought to the game. Their legacy is not just about what they achieved on the court, but how they made people feel, how they made the game of basketball a thrilling spectacle, a true showtime.

Made in the USA
Las Vegas, NV
08 January 2024

84101310R00075